Multicultural Projects Index

Multicultural Projects Index

Things to Make and Do to Celebrate Festivals, Cultures, and Holidays Around the World

Third Edition

Mary Anne Pilger

2002
LIBRARIES UNLIMITED
A Division of Greenwood Publishing Group, Inc.
Englewood, Colorado

Libraries Unlimited
A Division of Greenwood Publishing Group, Inc.
P.O. Box 6633
Englewood, CO 80155-6633
1-800-237-6124
www.lu.com

Library of Congress Cataloging-in-Publication Data

Pilger, Mary Anne.
   Multicultural projects index : things to make and do to celebrate festivals, cultures, and
holidays around the world / Mary Anne Pilger.-- 3rd ed.
     p. cm.
   Includes bibliographical references and index.
   ISBN 1-56308-898-3 (cloth)
    1. Multicultural education--Bibliography. 2. Multicultural education--Activity
programs--Indexes. 3. Festivals--Indexes. 4. Handicrafts--Indexes. 5. Games--Indexes. I.
Title.

Z5814.M86 P55 2001
[LC1099]
016.370117--dc21

2001054446

Contents

Dedication

I dedicate this book to my son, Charlie, whose love and encouragement sustains my life.

Acknowledgments

Many thanks to Mary Ann Still for her marvelous typing skills and her tenacity to get the job done.

Introduction

Crafts or handicrafts, those things we create in our minds and make with our hands, have been the visible proof of humankind's existence on our Earth; the visible demonstrations of cultures, now and in the past; the visible proof of humankind's struggle to find its very reason for being; the visible proof that humans and their cultures are different and unique.

The drive to create, to make, is inherent to human interpretation of the world. Human creations, crafts, or handicrafts give us a window to observe lives we cannot live or know. Our fragile existence on this Earth is measured by what we create, what we do with what we have; and these creations leave a historical record for all to observe and interpret.

People, in their uniqueness, in their differences, and in their similarities, are what make the world's peoples so special. Before people can live in peace, there must be understanding, understanding that geography determines how they live and that their culture—their ethnic being—evolves from their need for survival and their need for self-expression. Adaptation to one's environment means providing food, clothing, and shelter. Adaptation to one's personal environment means providing customs for personal growth and creativity. Spiritual and family customs, language and speaking customs, music and dance customs, festival and holiday customs, folklore and games customs—these customs, from the most primitive tribes to our most sophisticated nations, arc what make us the same . . . and different.

We are now a country of many cultures, and our schools and classrooms are evidence of this. Almost every teacher today faces classrooms made up of children from many different cultural backgrounds.

Festivals, holidays, and family celebrations are no longer from our older traditional American celebrations only. Today educators need to know the importance and significance of cultural traditions from many countries, and they also need to know how to have all students understand the similarities and differences of these celebrations.

Books in this index represent a vast storehouse of knowledge and information about world cultures and their handicrafts. Each author is an artist bringing to his or her book an intensity and view based on his or her own personal inspiration to write a book about a particular handicraft from a particular culture or cultures.

Educators need the information that this multicultural projects index provides for crafts, clothing, and special activities for holiday celebrations and religious observances, such as the Mexican Cinco de Mayo, the Indian Holi Festival, the Japanese Boys Day Carp Festival, Fourth of July, in the United States.

Children's literature provides what is needed for classroom teachers to have meaningful programs; this index is a key to open the door to all this information in children's books.

Subject Headings

This listing contains all the subject headings used in the text. Consult the text for cross-references between headings. Entries marked with an asterisk can be found in the second edition of *Multicultural Projects Index* (Libraries Unlimited, 1998).

ABORIGINES
ABORIGINES—ART
ABORIGINES—BASKETS
ABORIGINES—
  BOOMERANGS
ABORIGINES—
  HANDICRAFTS
ABORIGINES—MESSAGE
  STICKS
ABORIGINES—MUSICAL
  INSTRUMENTS
ABORIGINES—PAINTINGS
ABORIGINES—STRING
  FIGURES
ABORIGINES—WEAPONS
ADDITIVES*
ADVENT
AESOP*
AFRICA
AFRICA—ANIMALS
AFRICA—BEADS
AFRICA—BOBO PEOPLE—
  MASKS
AFRICA—CLOTHING
AFRICA—COOKERY
AFRICA—FOLKLORE
AFRICA—GAMES
AFRICA—HANDICRAFTS
AFRICA—HOUSES
AFRICA—JEWELRY
AFRICA—MASKS
AFRICA—MUSIC
AFRICA—MUSICAL
  INSTRUMENTS
AFRICA—PAINTINGS
AFRICA—POTTERY
AFRICA—SHIELDS
AFRICA—TREES

AFRICA, CENTRAL—
  CREATURES
AFRICA, CENTRAL—HOUSES
AFRICA, CENTRAL—
  JEWELRY
AFRICA, EAST—BEADS
AFRICA, NORTH—
  COOKERY
AFRICA, WEST—CLOTH
AFRICA, WEST—CLOTHING
AFRICA, WEST—COOKERY
AFRICA, WEST—DOLLS
AFRICA, WEST—EASTER—
  COOKERY
AFRICA, WEST—FESTIVALS
AFRICA, WEST—
  FESTIVALS—COOKERY
AFRICA, WEST—
  FOLKLORE
AFRICA, WEST—GAMES
AFRICA, WEST—
  HANDICRAFTS
AFRICA, WEST—NAMES
AFRICA, WEST—TIE-DYE
AFRO-AMERICANS
AFRO-AMERICANS—BEADS
AFRO-AMERICANS—
  COOKERY
AFRO-AMERICANS—
  FESTIVALS
AFRO-AMERICANS—
  HANDICRAFTS
AFRO-AMERICANS—
  HISTORY—COOKERY
AFRO-AMERICANS—
  HISTORY—DOLLS
AFRO-AMERICANS—
  HISTORY—GAMES

AFRO-AMERICANS—
  HISTORY—TOYS
AGIKUYU (PEOPLE)—
  WEDDINGS—COOKERY
AITUTAKI ISLAND—
  FLANNEL BOARD
  STORIES
ALABAMA
ALABAMA—COOKERY
ALASKA
ALASKA—COOKERY
ALASKA—FESTIVALS
ALASKA—FLANNEL
  BOARD STORIES
ALEXANDER THE GREAT
ALGERIA—COOKERY
ALGONQUIN INDIANS
ALGONQUIN INDIANS—
  CLOTHING
ALGONQUIN INDIANS—
  COOKERY
ALGONQUIN INDIANS—
  FOLKLORE
ALGONQUIN INDIANS—
  GAMES
ALGONQUIN INDIANS—
  HEADBANDS
ALGONQUIN INDIANS—
  MUSICAL INSTRUMENTS
ALICE IN WONDERLAND
ALL FOOLS' DAY. *See*
  APRIL FOOLS' DAY
AMAZON INDIANS—
  HEADDRESSES
AMAZON JUNGLE—RAIN
  STICKS
AMAZON RIVER
AMERICAN HEART MONTH

Key to Index

The Index is arranged in the following order:

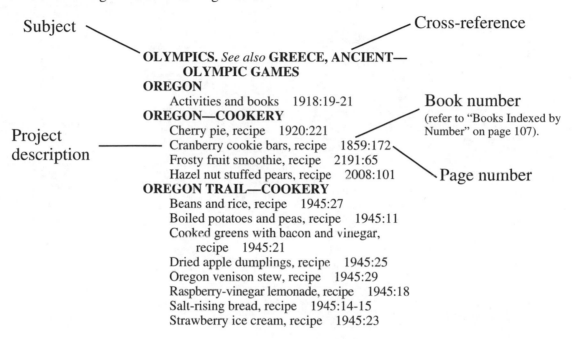

Subject

Cross-reference

OLYMPICS. *See also* **GREECE, ANCIENT—OLYMPIC GAMES**

OREGON
Activities and books   1918:19-21

Book number
(refer to "Books Indexed by Number" on page 107).

OREGON—COOKERY
Cherry pie, recipe   1920:221

Project description

Cranberry cookie bars, recipe   1859:172
Frosty fruit smoothie, recipe   2191:65
Hazel nut stuffed pears, recipe   2008:101

Page number

OREGON TRAIL—COOKERY
Beans and rice, recipe   1945:27
Boiled potatoes and peas, recipe   1945:11
Cooked greens with bacon and vinegar, recipe   1945:21
Dried apple dumplings, recipe   1945:25
Oregon venison stew, recipe   1945:29
Raspberry-vinegar lemonade, recipe   1945:18
Salt-rising bread, recipe   1945:14-15
Strawberry ice cream, recipe   1945:23

After finding a project of interest, check the book number in "Books Indexed by Number," page 107, to find the author, title, and publication data for the book in which the project is printed.

A

Note: Entries (including *see also* references) marked with an asterisk can be found in the second edition of *Multicultural Projects Index* (Libraries Unlimited, 1998).

ABORIGINES
  Grave carvings, oatmeal boxes, paints, making
    2139:49
ABORIGINES—ART
  Susan Wanji Wanji, Australian Aboriginal artist,
    how to copy her techniques   1770:26-29
ABORIGINES—BASKETS
  Bark basket, burlap or paper woven, paints, yarn,
    making   2139:50
ABORIGINES—BOOMERANGS
  Boomerang, cardboard, paint, making   2139:51
  Decorated cardboard boomerang, making
    1862:26-27
ABORIGINES—HANDICRAFTS
  Mini rug, hardware cloth, yarn, making   2054:140
  Yumbulul story design, T-shirt, fabric, crayons,
    making   2054:139
ABORIGINES—MESSAGE STICKS
  Message sticks, cardboard tube, making   2139:52
ABORIGINES—MUSICAL INSTRUMENTS
  Clap stick, making   1948:142
  Clapping sticks, wood pieces, paints, making
    1938:28-29
ABORIGINES—PAINTINGS
  Bark paintings, wood, paint, making   2139:52
  Dreamtime pareamtime painting, white paper,
    paints, making   2054:141
  Rock paintings, x-ray pictures, sandpaper, paint,
    making   2139:51
  X-ray painting, paper, paints, making   1915:15-17
ABORIGINES—STRING FIGURES
  Cat's cradle picture, yarn, paper, glue, making
    2139:52
ABORIGINES—WEAPONS
  Hand spear, paper, glue, making   2139:51
ADDITIVES.* *See also* **FOOD—JUNK FOOD**
ADVENT
  Advent boxes, 24 small boxes, wrapping paper,
    making   2055:133
AESOP.* *See also* **FABLES**
AFRICA
  Folk tales, celebrations, arts and crafts, foods, activ-
    ity pages, games   2201:1-41
AFRICA—ANIMALS
  African elephant picture, paper, paints, pattern,
    making   2139:74-75

  Jungle insects and birds pictures, making   2139:74
  Jungle snakes, pantyhose snake, paints, making
    2139:74
  Termite mounds cutout model or picture, pattern,
    making   2139:79
  Zebra prints, corrugated cardboard, paints, pattern,
    making   2139:76-77
AFRICA—BEADS
  Salt dough beads, making   2099:17
AFRICA—BOBO PEOPLE—MASKS
  Bobo mask, poster board, paper plates, making
    1948:89
AFRICA—CLOTHING
  Raffia grass dance skirts, paper, making   2139:66
AFRICA—COOKERY
  African fruit salad, recipe   2222:4
  Banana bread, recipe   2099:26-27
  Cocada amarela, coconut pudding, recipe   1784:177
  Fufu (New World version), recipe   2201:26
  Fufu dough for soups and stews, recipe   2201:25
  Fufu, recipe   2222:10
  Groundnut stew, recipe   2222:8
  Karringmelk beskuit, sweet buttermilk biscuits,
    recipe   1784:177
  Kulikuli, ground nut balls, recipe   1784:178
  Little yam cakes, recipe   2222:11
  Mafe, ground nut stew, recipe   1784:178
  Peanut sauce dish, recipe   2201:25
  Peanut soup, recipe   2099:8-9
  Spicy chicken drumsticks, recipe   2099:20-21
  Squash with peanuts, recipe   2099:16-17
  Sweet doughnut balls, recipe   2201:25
AFRICA—FOLKLORE
  How Frog Lost his Tail story with whole language
    activities   1768:3-9
AFRICA—GAMES
  Camel race, how to play 1948:179
  Mankala game, egg carton, dried beans, making
    2043:73-74
AFRICA—HANDICRAFTS
  Animal abstracts, twigs, natural materials, making
    2054:31
  Grigri charms, cork wall tiles, string, making
    2054:30
AFRICA—HOUSES
  Mud brick house, dirt, water, making   1910:21-22

B

BAKI. *See* **INDONESIA***

BALI—SHADOW PUPPETS
Shadow puppet, cardboard, sticks, paper fasteners, making 2140:28-29

BALKANS—HARVEST FESTIVALS—DOLLS
Corn doll, dried grass or raffia, lace, making 1846:19

BALLET—JEWELRY
Ballet dancer pin, craft sticks, embroidery thread, making 1820:9-11

BAMILEKE (AFRICAN PEOPLE)—MASKS
Animals masks, plaster of Paris, markers, making 2054:14

BANGLADESH—FLAG
Pattern of flag 1948:42-43

BARK RUBBINGS. *See also* **RUBBINGS***

BAROTSE (AFRICAN PEOPLE)—BASKETS
Colorful baskets, fabric, making 2054:15

BASKETRY. *See also* **INDIANS OF NORTH AMERICA—BASKETRY***

BATIK
Paste batik, muslin, recipe for paste, making 2055:143
Wax resist technique for batik, how to do 2212:155-157

BATS
Tales about bats and their characteristics 2060:7-9

BAUM, L. FRANK. *See also* **WIZARD OF OZ***

BEACH. *See also* **SEASHORE**

BEACH—FLANNEL BOARD STORIES
Felt stories and activities, character patterns, felt board and stand, making 1827:107-115

BEADS. *See also* **JEWELRY***
Bead threading tray, ceiling tile, bottle top, making 1871:29
Beading loom, how to build and use, wood, nails, thread 1875:168-171
Clay beads, making 1948:82
Clay dough beads, recipe for dough, making 2055:223
Colored pasta beads, making 1948:81
Enameled pendants, plastic granules, silver wire, making 1871:10-11
Paper beads, making 1948:83-84
Rose bead necklace, making 1973:11
Salt and flour beads, recipe 2184:145
Trading beads, millefiori technique, plastic modeling material, making 1871:8-9

BEADWORK. *See also* **INDIANS OF NORTH AMERICA—BEADWORK**

BEASTS. *See* **MONSTERS**

BEAUTY AND THE BEAST
Beauty, the Beast, fabric, patterns, making 1793:7-8

BELARUS—COOKERY
Stuffed beef cutlets, recipe 2068:119

BELL, ALEXANDER GRAHAM
Activities from easy to difficult to study his life 2018:2-47

BENIN—HOUSES
Stilt houses picture, paper, toothpicks, making 2139:64

BENIN—STORY BANNERS
Cloth story banner, fabric, paper, thread, making 2136:23-25

BIBLE—HANDICRAFTS
Baby Jesus in the manger, making 2084:20
Baby Jesus, making 2084:20
Basket with five loaves and two fishes, paper plate, yarn, making 2146:46-48
Basket with multiplying loaves and fish, making 2084:23
Bible school memory frames, making 2084:22
Burning bush, making 2084:5
Circle and cross pendant and key ring, making 2084:17
Coat of many colors bookmark, making 2084:4
Creation flower paperweight, making 2084:1
Creation wheel, cardboard, markers, making 2146:8-9
Cross from plastic canvas, making 2084:9
Daniel's lacing lion, making 2084:11
David and Goliath puppets, making 2084:6
Doily angel, making 2084:18
Empty tomb, paper bowls, aluminum foil, making 2146:58-59
Faith pennant, making 2084:28
Fish friendship bracelets, making 2084:27
Fishers of men wall hanging, making 2084:22
Glow in the dark angel, making 2084:19
Hair-growing Samson, egg carton, soil, grass seed, making 2145:26-27
Handwriting appears on the wall, paper, making 2146:34-35
Jacob's ladder, egg cartons, foil cups, making 2146:16-17

Jesus ascends, matchbox, fiberfill, string, making 2146:62-63

Jesus walks on water, blue paper, making 2146:52-53

Joseph and his coat of many colors magnet, pipe cleaners, yarn, beads, making 2146:18-19

Joyful noisemaker, making 2084:8

Lamb and lion magnets, making 2084:10

Lamb, paper, cotton balls, ribbon, making 2146:28-29

Let it shine candle, making 2084:7

Manger, cardboard tube, poster board, making 2146:38-39

Moses in the bulrushes model, making 2084:4

Mustard seed bookmark, making 2084:1

Noah's Ark bag tag, making 2084:2

Noah's Ark model, paper plates, paper, making 2146:12-13

Noah's Ark rainbow, making 2084:2

Parting of the Red Sea, cardboard, sand, blue plastic wrap, making 2146:22-23

Paul over the wall, plastic berry basket, cardboard, yarn, making 2146:62-63

Praise pennant, making 2084:28

Raising Jairus' daughter, making 2084:24

Ram horn trumpet, party horn, paper, yarn, making 2146:24-25

Resurrection mobile, making 2084:21

Shadrach, Meshach and Abednego in the fiery furnace, oatmeal box, tissue paper, foil, making 2146:32-33

Stand up and walk, paper, markers, making 2146:44-45

Standing sheep, making 2084:7

Story about gratitude, paper, markers, making 2146:54-55

Symbols of faith bookmarks, making 2084:21

Symbols of faith craft foam stamps, making 2084:12

Ten commandments booklet, making 2084:5

Tower of Babel model, making 2084:3

Tree of knowledge, pipe stems, beads, yarn, making 2146:10-11

Turning water into wine, paper plates, paints, making 2146:42-43

Waving palms, paper plates, markers, making 2146:56-57

Who's in the tree, making 2084:25

Who's in the whale, making 2084:25

BIBLE—HATS

Three Kings hats, party hats, styrofoam balls, yarn, making 2146:40-41

BIBLE—PUPPETS

Elijah and the ravens puppets, making 2146:30-31

Jairus's daughter puppet, tube sock, salt box, fabric, making 2146:49-51

Jonah in the big fish puppet, socks, yarn, making 2146:36-37

Moses in the bulrushes glove puppet, egg carton, felt, yarn, glove, making 2146:20-21

Sarah and Baby Isaac puppets, felt, old mitten, making 2145:14-15

BIRTHDAYS

Science, language arts, art, music, math and social studies activities 2163:13-30

BIRTHDAYS—SONGS

Happy Birthday to you song in Arabic, French, German, Hebrew, Italian, Korean, Portuguese and Spanish 1749:46-47

BLACKFOOT INDIANS—BEADWORK

Beaded headband, felt, beads, ribbon, colored pencils, making 1762:18-23

BLACKFOOT INDIANS—GAMES

Snow hopping game, how to play 1948:214

BOBO (AFRICAN PEOPLE)—MASKS

Bobo mask, poster board, paper plates, making 1948:89

BOLIVIA—COOKERY

Humitas, tamales, recipe 1784:184

BOLIVIA—FESTIVALS—COOKERY

Alacitas Fair; edible miniature, recipe 2054:155

Candelaria Day; stuffed avocado, recipe 1810:11

Lent Devil's Carnival; chicken pie with corn topping, recipe 1810:15

BOLIVIA—HANDICRAFTS

Clay truck, clay, paints, making 1810:18-19

Fabric appliqued picture, making 1810:24-25

BOLIVIA—LANGUAGE

Greetings from Bolivia in Spanish 1810:7

BOOKS

Motion picture flip book, pad, markers, making 2054:13-16

Quilted book cover, cardboard, fabric, making 1918:208-211

Sketchbook with secret compartment, making 1868:65-68

Starburst collection book bound in a lotus book form, making 1868:90-93

BORNEO. *See also* **INDONESIA**

BOSNIA–HERZEGOVINA. *See* **YUGOSLAVIA**

BOWLS. *See also* **CLAY; POTTERY; INDIANS OF NORTH AMERICA—POTTERY***

BRADFORD, WILLIAM

Activities from easy to difficult to study the life of William Bradford 2198:1-43

BRAIDING. *See also* **STRING FIGURES***

BRAMBLY HEDGE

Dust Dogwood soft toy, fabrics, felt, patterns, making 1869:41-48

Mrs. Apple soft toy, fabrics, felt, ribbons, lace, patterns, making 1869:29-40

Poppy Eyebright soft toy, fabrics, felt, lace, silk, patterns, making 1869:49-64

Primrose wood mouse soft toy, fabrics, ribbons, lace, patterns, making 1869:11-20

Wilfred Toadflax soft toy, fabrics, felt, patterns, making 1869:21-28

BRAZIL

Songs, stories, rhymes, puppets, crafts, patterns 2231:15-31

BRAZIL—BIRTHDAYS—DECORATIONS

Flowers, colored tissue paper, pipe cleaners, making 1749:10-11

BRAZIL—CHRISTMAS—COOKERY

Rabanadas, French toast like dessert, recipe 1813:27

BRAZIL—COOKERY

Avocado soup, recipe 1751:83-84

Meat and mashed potato pie, recipe 2099:118-119

Pudim custard dessert, recipe 1751:85

Shrimp with corn, recipe 1751:84

Sweet milk candy, recipe 2099:126-127

BRAZIL—FESTIVALS—COOKERY

Bonfim Festival; black bean soup, recipe 2167:29

Bumba Bull Festival; mimini fish, recipe 2167:21

Carnival; meat stew, recipe 1900:19-21

Carnival; orange salad, recipe 1900:18-19

Carnival; pepper scented rice, recipe 2167:17

Carnival; shredded greens, recipe 1900:22-23

Goddess Festival; black beans, recipe 1900:30-31

Goddess Festival; codfish with onion, garlic and tomatoes, recipe 1900:28-29

Goddess Festival; grape tapioca pudding, recipe 1900:32-33

Saint John's Day; peanut brittle (pe-de-moleque), recipe 1813:19

Saint John's Day; pineapple orange drink, recipe 1900:42

Saint John's Day; sweet popcorn, recipe 1900:38-39

Saint John's Day; sweet potato and coconut balls, recipe 1900:40-41

Saint John's Day; corn cake, recipe 2167:25

BRAZIL—FESTIVALS—COSTUMES

Carnival costumes, pillowcases, fabric, making 2054:156

BRAZIL—FESTIVALS—HANDICRAFTS

Carnival Amazon headdress, paper, raffia, beads, feathers, making 1813:16-17

Carnival Samba dancers, wire, decorations, making 2054:157

BRAZIL—FESTIVALS—MASKS

Carnival mask, pattern, making 2231:31

BRAZIL—FESTIVALS—MUSICAL INSTRUMENTS

June Festival maracas; balloon, papier mache, rice, making 1813:20-21

BRAZIL—FESTIVALS—SONGS

Saint John's Day traditional song, Fall, Fall, Balloon (Cai Cai Balao) 1813:21

BRAZIL—GAMES

Penny on a post, how to make and play 1948:176

BRAZIL—HANDICRAFTS

Anaconda snake sculpture, sheet, wire, making 2054:167

Hemp rope figure, hemp, rope, wire, making 2054:159

BRAZIL—INDIANS

Tembe Indian headdress, brown bag, paper, straws, feathers, making 1948:56-58

BRAZIL—JEWELRY

Picture necklace, beads, yarn, making 1948:114

BRAZIL—MUSICAL INSTRUMENTS

Flute; drinking straw flute, feathers, yarn, making 2054:158

BRAZIL—NEW YEAR'S DAY—HANDICRAFTS

New Year's card, making 2014:44-45

BRAZIL—RAIN FOREST

Great Kapok Tree dramatization; stage, marionettes, animals and human patterns, making 1867:23-26

BREAD

Bread from wheat berries, recipe 2125:15-17

History of bread around the world 1775:4-9

Modern sourdough starter, recipe 1950:18

Sourdough bread, recipe 1950:19

BREWSTER, SIR DAVID

Kaleidoscope, mylar plastic, tape, making 2054:102

BRICKS

Brick making, how to do 2055:244

BRITISH ISLES. *See also* **ENGLAND; IRELAND; SCOTLAND; WALES**

BRUEGEL, PIETER

Bruegel type pictures of crowds, making 2050:16-17

BUBBLES

World's best bubbles, recipe 2211:33

BUCKAROOS. *See* **COWBOYS**

BUDDHA—FESTIVALS

New Years Losar bunting prayer flags, fabric, string, making 1846:11

BUDDHISM—COOKERY

Noodles with tofu, recipe 1772:17

BUDDHISM—MANDALA

Mandala, cardboard, colored glitter, glue, making 1772:23

BUDDHISM—SYMBOLS

Lotus flower, pink, white and green paper, making 1772:21

BURCHFIELD, CHARLES

Burchfield pictures in wintry colors, making 2047:24-25

BURKINA FASO—GAMES

Chess pieces, make from clay, plaster of Paris, pipe cleaners, how to play 1870:26-27

BURMA. *See also* **MYANMAR***

BURNE-JONES, EDWARD

King Arthur stained glass picture, picture of jewels, window hanging, making 2048:24-25

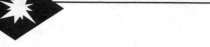

C

CACTI
Cactus table decoration, plastic cup, cardboard, making 2147:10-11
Prickly pear cactus pattern 2227:71
Saguaro cactus pattern 2227:75

CACTI—PUPPETS
Expanding cactus puppet, sock, oatmeal box, making 2147:8-9

CALDER, ALEXANDER
Calder mobile, wire, styrofoam, paper, making 2054:129
Create mobile like Alexander Calder 2184:94-97

CALIFORNIA. *See also* **INDIANS OF NORTH AMERICA—CALIFORNIA***
Activities and books 1918:21-23

CALIFORNIA—COOKERY
Bean and cheese burritos, recipe 1781:84
Caesar salad, recipe 1859:166
California date walnut bread, recipe 1789:161
Gazpacho soup, recipe 1968:94
Graham cracker cookies, recipe 1920:177

CAMBODIA—FESTIVALS—COOKERY
Kan Ben Festival; bananas cooked in coconut milk, recipe 1823:23
Royal Plowing Festival; fruit salad, recipe 1823:19

CAMBODIA—FESTIVALS—HANDICRAFTS
Water Festival; houseboat, colored paper, skewer sticks, making 1823;28-29

CAMBODIA—FESTIVALS—KITES
Full Moon Festival; kite, colored paper, skewer sticks, making 1823:24-25

CAMBODIA—HANDICRAFTS
Story banner, fabric, crayons, making 2054:54

CAMEROON—HOUSES
Mud brick house, dirt, water, making 1910:21-22

CAMEROON—MASKS
Animal masks, plaster of Paris, markers, making 2054:14

CAMPING. *See also* **TRAILBLAZING***

CANADA
Activities and books 1918:135-144
Folk tales, celebrations, arts and crafts, foods, activity pages, games 2201:125-160
Maple leaf pattern 2227:39

CANADA—BIRTHDAYS—DECORATIONS
Crackers party favors, toilet paper tubes, tissue paper, ribbon, making 1749:12-13

CANADA—COOKERY
Blueberry pudding, recipe 2099:104-105
Butter tarts, recipe 1926:248
Gingerbread, recipe 2201:144-145
Grilled cheese and Canadian bacon sandwiches, recipe 2201:145
Hot chocolate, recipe 2201:145
Nanaimo bars, recipe 1926:230-231
Poires Helene (pears Helen), recipe 2201:146
Prairie berry cake, recipe 1811:96-98
Sourdough biscuits, recipe 2201:144
Sourdough starter, recipe 2201:144
Toad in the hole, recipe 1926:24

CANADA—HANDICRAFTS
Maple leaf printing, clay, red paint, leaves, making 2054:112

CANADA—INDIANS. *See also* **KWAKIUTL INDIANS; MICMAC INDIANS***

CANADA—SCULPTURE
Inuit-style sculpture, plaster of Paris, vermiculite, paint, making 2033:30

CANADA DAY—COOKERY
Firecracker ice cream dessert, recipe 2185:85
Maple leaf sugar cookies, recipe 2185:84

CANADA DAY—DECORATIONS
Badge, heavy paper, ribbon, pattern, making 2206:32

CANDLEHOLDERS
Ready to eat candleholders, recipe 2185:152

CANDLES
Beeswax candles, making 2161:102-103
Drip candles, wax, wick, making 2184:67
History of candle making 2163:162-163
Ice candles, wax, ice, wick, making 2184:67
Sand candles, sand, wax, wick, making 2184:65
Shell candles, shells, wax, wick, making 2184:66
Whipped wax candles, wax, wick, making 2184:67

CANOES. *See also* **INDIANS OF NORTH AMERICA—CANOES**

CAPE COD—COOKERY
Oatmeal cookies, recipe 1926:226-227

CAREERS. *See also* **Individual Occupations**

CARIBBEAN ISLANDS
Folk tales, celebrations, arts and crafts, foods, activity pages, games 2201:161-194
Songs, stories, rhymes, puppets, crafts, patterns 2231:33-46

CARIBBEAN ISLANDS—COOKERY
Callaloo soup, recipe 2222:16

Calypso coconut chicken, recipe 2222:19
Candied sweet potatoes, recipe 2004:19
Chocolate sponge, recipe 2201:181
Cuban black bean soup, recipe 2201:180
Curried coconut vegetables, recipe 2222:21
Curried lamb, recipe 2004:15
Date and nut bars, recipe 2201:181
Figues bananes fourrees, banana dessert, recipe 2201:178
Fried chicken, recipe 2004:25
Island banana fritters, recipe 2222:22
Island fruit smoothies drink, recipe 2222:23
Oven-fried yams, recipe 2222:18
Pineapple coconut balls, recipe 2201:179
Pineapple drink, recipe 2201:178
Pineapple snow, recipe 2222:23
Rice, Caribbean-style, recipe 1745:28-29
Saltfish cakes, recipe 2004:29
Shrimp boats, recipe 2201:179

CARIBBEAN ISLANDS—MUSICAL INSTRUMENTS
Maracas, light bulbs, papier mache, making 2054:115
Maracas, plastic bottles, beans, making 1812:98-100

CARLE, ERIC
Activities using Eric Carle picture books 2095:184-189

CARNIVAL—MASKS
Bird mask and collar, cardboard, shiny paper, making 1829:28-29

CARNIVALS. See also **MARDI GRAS**
CAROUSELS. See also **MERRY-GO-ROUNDS***
CARPENTRY. See **WOODWORKING***
CARS. See **AUTOMOBILES***
CARVER, GEORGE WASHINGTON—COOKERY
Homemade peanut butter, recipe 2030:109

CARVER, GEORGE WASHINGTON— HANDICRAFTS
Peanut butter play dough, making 2030:108

CARVING. See also **STONE CARVING; WOOD CARVING***
Soap carved sculpture, making 1875:198

CASTLES
Cookie dough castle, pattern, recipe 2085:28-31
Mangonel catapult, wood, nails, rubber bands, clay, cannon ball, making 1860:9
Turret, turrets and walls, finishing touches, making 1979:27-33

CASTLES—COOKERY
Peas pottage, green peas, milk, recipe 2135:33

CASTLES—GARDENS
Herb garden, how to plant 2135:19

CASTLES—WEAVING
Tapestry, how to weave your own, cardboard, wool, yarn, making 2135:29

CATS—PUPPETS
Stick cat puppet, stick, cardboard, paints, making 1764:16-17

CAVEMEN—BREAD
History of bread 1950:7

CELTS. See also **DRUIDS***
CELTS—JEWELRY
Celt brooch, poster board, decorations, pattern, making 2231:163-165

CENTRAL AMERICA. See also **LATIN AMERICA**
CENTRAL AMERICA—INDIANS. See also **CUNA INDIANS**
CENTRAL AMERICA—MASKS
Crocodile mask, poster board, crayons, pattern, making 2109:59

CENTRAL ASIA—FELT
Felt balls, jewelry, wall hangings, figures, fleece, carded wool, knitted wool, making 2200:10-11

CEYLON. See also **SRI LANKA***
CHAD—FLAG
Pattern of flag 1948:42-43

CHAGALL, MARC
Slumbering Titania watercolor picture in Chagall style, making 2051:24-25

CHAINS. See also **PAPER CHAINS***
CHALK
Sidewalk chalk, recipe 2211:43
Spray chalk, recipe 2211:57

CHANUKAH. See **HANUKKAH**
CHAPMAN, JOHN. See also **JOHNNY APPLESEED**
CHEROKEE INDIANS—FOLKLORE
The Ball Game story with whole language activities 1768:26-32

CHEROKEE INDIANS—GAMES
Chunkey game, how to make and play 2101:43
Hoop and pole game, how to play 2075:22

CHEYENNE INDIANS—COOKERY
Cheyenne batter bread, recipe 1786:81
Cheyenne batter bread, recipe 1859:149

CHEYENNE INDIANS—FOLKLORE
Her Seven Brothers by Paul Goble, shadow puppet theater, story characters patterns, how to do play 2060:39-48

CHEYENNE INDIANS—MYTHOLOGY
Myth of the Great Spirit magic shield, making 2048:20
Myth of the Great Spirit picture of the Great Spirit, making 2048:21
Myth of the Great Spirit storm of birds, making 2048:21

CHILDREN'S BOOK DAY
Activities to celebrate National Children's Book Day 1791:128-131

CHILDREN'S BOOK WEEK
Activities, crafts 1990:67-70
Activities, crafts 1991:63-66
Activities, crafts 1992:63-66

D

E

ESKIMOS—CARVING
Ivory carving from cardboard, black crayon, making   2213:4-5
ESKIMOS—CLOTHING
Mittens, felt, cotton, wool, ribbon, making   2213:14-15
ESKIMOS—COOKERY
Nanook's homemade ice cream, recipe   2201:146
ESKIMOS—GAMES
Ajaga; cup and ball game, make from clay, how to play   1870:16-17
Ptarmigan against ducks game, how to play   1948:214
Run around the igloo, game for spinning top   1948:70
Stuffed animal blanket toss game, how to play   1948:184
Throwing game with clay animals, how to make and play   2213:22-23
ESKIMOS—HOUSES
Igloos picture or eggshell igloo, making   2139:205
Snow house model, papier mache, balloon, white paint, making   2213:20-21
ESKIMOS—JEWELRY
Whale tooth necklaces, styrofoam whale tooth, making   2139:211
ESKIMOS—MASKS
Laughing masks, making   1885:40-41
ESKIMOS—SCULPTURE
Inuit animal sculpture, dough, paints, making   1812:53-55
Inuit-style sculpture, plaster of Paris, vermiculite, paint, making   2033:30
ESKIMOS—SLEDS
Model sled, balsa wood, cardboard, fabric scraps, making   2213:8-9
ESKIMOS—SNOW GOGGLES
Snow goggles, poster board, making   2063:22
ESKIMOS—TOYS
Inuit Inapaq yo-yo, spool, fur, seeds, yarn, making   1934:77-79
ETHIOPIA—COOKERY
Chicken stew, luku, recipe   2222:6
Cowboy coffee cake, recipe   1920:15
Injera, recipe   1811:31-33
Kale and potatoes, recipe   2222:9
Kanya sweetmeat, recipe   1916:44
Oxtail soup, recipe   1916:44
ETHIOPIA—EASTER—COOKERY
Fasika; lentil stew, recipe   1897:23

ETHIOPIA—FOLKLORE
Fire on the Mountain by Jane Kurtz, activities and recipes for the classroom   1916:43-44
ETHIOPIA—LANGUAGE
Greetings from Ethiopia   1897:7
ETHIOPIA—PAINTINGS
Vellum old-time painting, chamois leather, paints, making   1897:28-29
ETHIOPIA—RELIGION—CROSSES
Plaster and silver paint cross, clay, yarn, making   1897:20-21
EUROPE
Folk tales, celebrations, arts and crafts, foods, activity pages, games   2201:195-236
EUROPE—BREAD
History of bread   1950:34
EUROPE—CHRISTMAS—COOKERY
Moravian Christmas bread, recipe   1950:84-85
EUROPE—COOKERY
Borscht soup, recipe   2201:219
Mazurkas dessert, recipe   2201:219
Pappilan hatavara (bread pudding), recipe   2201:218
Pretzels, recipe   1950:35
Salata salad, recipe   2201:218
Zupa jablkowa (apple snow), recipe   2201:219
Zupa z dynia (pumpkin soup), recipe   2201:218
EUROPE—GAMES
Dominoes, make from wood or clay, how to play   1870:14-15
Jacks, make from clay or pebbles, how to play   1870:10-11
Spinning top, make from CD and knitting needle, how to play   1870:12-13
EXPLORATION
Historical literature, activities, crafts, foods, recipes   2113:25-26
EXPLORATION—HISTORICAL FICTION
I Sailed with Columbus by Miriam Schlein, activities, crafts, foods, recipes   2113:38-40
If You Were There in 1492 by Barbara Brenner, activities, crafts, foods, recipes   2113:27-31
Pedro's Journal by Pam Conrad, activities, crafts, foods, recipes   2113:25-27
The Tainos by Francine Jacobs, activities, crafts, foods, recipes   2113:34-37
Voyage of the Half Moon by Tracey West, activities, crafts, foods, recipes   2113:40-41
Around the World in a Hundred Years by Jean Fritz, activities, crafts, foods, recipes   2113:31-34
EYE OF GOD. *See* **GOD'S EYE**

F

FABERGE EGGS
Faberge type jeweled egg, balloon, papier mache, decorations, making 1846:14
FABERGE, PETER CARL
Faberge decorated eggs, how to do 1765:4-5
Faberge type decorated egg, paints, glitter, foil, making 1738:26
Jeweled eggs, eggs, sequins, glitter, thread, making 2054:101
FACE MAKEUP. *See also* **MAKEUP***
FAIRY RINGS
Crocus bulb fairy ring, how to plant and grow 1973:34
FALL. *See also* **AUTUMN; LEAVES*; PUMPKINS**
Activities and patterns for primary or preschool projects 2204:1-44
FALSE FACE SOCIETY. *See also* **IROQUOIS INDIANS—MASKS**
FAMILY TREE
Family tree for gift, poster board, pattern for tree, making 2185:98-99
FANTE (AFRICAN PEOPLE)—FLAGS
Fante people patchwork flags, how to copy technique 1770:22-25
FARMS—COOKERY
Farmhouse cake, recipe 1798:59
FAST FOOD. *See* **FOOD—FAST FOOD***
FASTS AND FEASTS. *See* **FESTIVALS** *under* **Individual Countries**
FATHER'S DAY
Activities to celebrate 1791:160-163
Activities to celebrate 1993:83-86
Activities, crafts 1990:83-86
Activities, crafts 1991:83-86
Activities, crafts 1992:83-86
Activities, crafts 1994:83-86
Science, language arts, art, music, math and social studies activities 2163:331-346
FATHER'S DAY—COOKERY
Blueberry muffins, recipe 2185:76
Dad's day dessert tie, recipe 2053:160
Sweet rolls, recipe 1790:54-55
FATHER'S DAY—DECORATIONS
Bookmark, clear adhesive plastic, magazine pictures, making 2128:71-72
Lettered card, old card, magazine picture, making 2128:68-70
Turn-wheel card, paper, pencils, making 1790:53

FATHER'S DAY—FICTION
Hooray for Father's Day! By Marjorie Sharmat, activities, patterns, crafts 2183:58-63
FATHER'S DAY—HANDICRAFTS
Memo holder, craft sticks, paints, making 2185:78
Paperweight, glass jar, paints, glitter, making 2087:84
FAWKES, GUY. *See also* **ENGLAND—FESTIVALS**
FEAST OF LIGHTS. *See also* **HANUKKAH**
FESTIVAL OF LIGHT. *See* **SWEDEN— CHRISTMAS***
FIJI—HANDICRAFTS
Coral watercolor, paper, watercolor paint, making 2054:145
Stuffed cod hanging, paper, paints, yarn, making 2054:144
FINLAND—ANIMALS
Reindeer picture, making 2139:189
FINLAND—CHRISTMAS—DECORATIONS
Christmas gnome (Tontut), red napkin, felt, making 2203:27
Gnome's hat, red and green felt, making 2203:28-29
FINLAND—CHRISTMAS—HANDICRAFTS
Straw goat figure, wheat or grass stalks, making 1934:24
FINLAND—EASTER—COOKERY
Shrove Tuesday buns, recipe 2203:30-31
FINLAND—EASTER—DECORATIONS
Finnish Easter scene with baby wool ball chickens, making 2203:26
FINLAND—FOLKLORE
Aili's Quilt; patterns, making 1821:24-26
FINLAND—HANDICRAFTS
Lapland felt square, felt, fabric scraps, making 2054:94
FINLAND—QUILTING
Aili's Quilt; patterns, making 1821:24-26
FINLAND—SEASONS
Snow picture, making 2139:190
FIRE PREVENTION WEEK—HANDICRAFTS
Firefighter down the pole, tube, foil, yarn, making 2151:36-37
FIRE—FOLKLORE
Tales about human survival of fire 2060:10-12
FIRST NATIONS PEOPLES. *See* **INUIT INDIANS; ESKIMOS; HURON INDIANS***
FISH—COOKERY
Fish dishes from around the world 1777:24-25
History of eating fish around the world 1777:6-7

27

28

Crepe Fruzette fruit dessert, recipe   2225:125
Crepes, recipe   1784:181
Crepes, recipe   1926:42-43
Fish en Papillote, recipe   2222:42
French Baguette bread, recipe   1950:75
French bread, recipe   2027:31
French onion soup, recipe   2222:40
French toast, recipe   1950:79
French toast, recipe   2201:265
Garlic mayonnaise, recipe   2019:39
Pain Decore, French decorated bread, recipe
   2053:26
Potage parmentier, leek soup, recipe   2019:49
Potato cheese souffle, recipe   2222:45
Potato soup, cold, recipe   1797:23
Quiche Lorraine, recipe   2222:43
Raspberry sorbet dessert, recipe   2222:48
Ratatouille, recipe   2222:41
Salad Nicoise, recipe   2222:44
Senegalaise, chicken dish, recipe   2199:145
Strawberry crepes, recipe   2222:49
Sweet plum tart dessert, recipe   2222:47
Tomato soup with meatballs, recipe   2201:266
Tomatoes a la Provencale, recipe   1999:23
Vichyssoise, recipe   1933:35

FRANCE—EASTER—COOKERY
Provence-style kebabs, recipe   1907:23

FRANCE—FESTIVALS—COOKERY
Fete des Remparts; apple tart, recipe   1912:25
Lemon Festival; lemon mousse, recipe   1907:28
Shrove Tuesday; crepes, recipe   1907:19

FRANCE—FOLKLORE
Cinderella; creative ideas and projects   1909:1-27
Diamonds and Toads flannel board story, felt,
   patterns given   1767:94-97

FRANCE—FOLKLORE—DOLLS
Beauty and the Beast flip doll, beast to prince flip
   doll, paper, paints, making   1763:40-41
Cinderella rags to riches flip doll, fabric scraps,
   trims, making   1763:22-23

FRANCE—FOLKLORE—HANDICRAFTS
Puss in Boots box puzzle, small boxes, paper,
   markers, making   1763:20-21

FRANCE—FOLKLORE—PUPPETS
Sleeping Beauty wake up puppet, salt carton,
   fabric, paints, yarn, making   1763:46-47

FRANCE—GAMES
Marble bridge game, make from shoe box, how
   to play   1870:8-9
Wall marble game, how to play   1948:172

FRANCE—GEOGRAPHY
Chalk country, chalk hills picture, blue paper,
   white chalk, making   2139:125

FRANCE—GYPSIES—COOKERY
Fried cheese and ham sandwich, croque monsieur,
   recipe   1912:13

FRANCE—HANDICRAFTS
Flowers; paper pulp and paper flowers, making
   1808:18
Silhouette, black paper, chalk, making   2054:82
Soap; handmade soap, leftover soap, perfumes,
   making   2054:81

FRANCE—LANGUAGE
A few French words   1957:28

FRANCE—LAUNDRIES
Outdoor laundries mural, paper, paints, making
   2139:123

FRANCE—MUSICAL INSTRUMENTS
Tambourine; cardboard, bells, making   1912:16-17

FRANCE—PERFUMES
Perfume, homemade perfume, flower petals,
   grape seed oil, making   2139:126

FRANCE—PIGEON TOWERS
Pigeon cotes, small towers in fields, cardboard
   box model, making   2139:129

FRANCE—STAINED GLASS
Stained glass for window, plastic wrap, paints,
   making   2140:16-17

FRANCE—TOYS
Bagatelle pinball machine, board, nails, rubber
   bands, making   1934:149-150

FRANCE—VILLAGES
Door picture, poster board, paints, making   2139:129
Shop front picture, poster board, paints, making
   2139:130

FRANCE—VINEYARDS
Vineyards picture, green paper, purple paint,
   making   2139:123

FRANCE—WIGS
Wigs, paper bag wig, making   2139:127

FRANKLIN, BENJAMIN
Activities to learn about the life of Benjamin
   Franklin   1849:3-46

FREMONT INDIAN PEOPLE—FIGURINES
Fremont clay figurine, clay, making   2110:8-9

FREMONT INDIAN PEOPLE—PETROGLYPHS
Petroglyph book covers, paper, cord, paints,
   making   2110:14-15

FRIENDSHIP BRACELETS. *See* **GUATEMALA—
   HANDICRAFTS***

FRIENDSHIP DAY
Activities, crafts   1990:91-94
Activities, crafts   1991:91-94
Activities, crafts   1992:91-94

FRIENDSHIP MONTH—COOKERY
Jalapeno bagels, recipe   1790:17

FRIENDSHIP MONTH—DECORATIONS
Friendship mosaic, egg cartons, confetti, making
   1790:12

FRONTIER AND PIONEER LIFE. *See also*
   WILDER, LAURA INGALLS
Activities, literature, family history   1885:13-33

G

GA (AFRICAN PEOPLE)—FUNERALS
Lion coffin, boxes, pipe cleaners, wool, making 1846:30
GAMBIA—FESTIVALS—COOKERY
Id-ul-Fitr; chicken yussa, recipe 1819:17
GAMES. *See also* **Individual Topics**
GENEALOGY. *See* **FAMILY TREE**
GEORGIA
Activities and books 1918:111-122
GEORGIA—COOKERY
Fried pies, recipe 1920:209
Hot chicken souffle, recipe 1920:93
Peach pie, recipe 2100:73
Peanut butter and banana bread, recipe 1859:62
GEORGIA (SOVIET UNION)—COOKERY
Shasklyk, lamb meat dish, recipe 1760:118
GERMANIC PEOPLE. *See* **NORSEMEN***
GERMANY—BIRTHDAYS—HANDICRAFTS
Life candle, candle, stickers, sequins, string, making 1749:20-21
GERMANY—BIRTHDAYS—SONGS
Happy Birthday song to you in German 1749:46-47
GERMANY—CHRISTMAS—COOKERY
Gingerbread cookies, recipe 1924:13
Marzipan candy, recipe 2185:143
GERMANY—CHRISTMAS—HANDICRAFTS
Advent calendar, felt, yarn, wooden pole, making 1924:9
GERMANY—COOKERY
Bavarian sausage hot pot, recipe 2222:55
Bratwurst with sauerkraut and apples, recipe 2222:57
Bratwurst, recipe 1811:66-68
Cinnamon apple pancakes, recipe 2222:54
Crispy potato pancakes, recipe 2222:56-57
Flaky apple strudel, recipe 2222:58
Lemon pie, recipe 1920:207
Mini ham and cheese sandwiches, recipe 2222:55
Pfeffernuesse cookies, recipe 2199:161
Potato pancakes (Kartoffelpuffer), recipe 2201:265
Soft cookies, recipe 2201:267
Spaetzel dumplings, recipe 1919:15
Spaetzel noodles, recipe 2222:56
Thumbprint cookies, recipe 2222:59
GERMANY—DOLLS
Peddler doll, plastic bottle, panty hose, fabric, making 1807:10

GERMANY—EASTER—COOKERY
Almond paste eggs, recipe 1924:21
GERMANY—EASTER—HANDICRAFTS
Papier mache decorated eggs, making 1924:23
GERMANY—FESTIVALS—COOKERY
Carnival (Fasching); fried ring doughnuts, recipe 1924:19
GERMANY—FOLKLORE
Diamonds and Toads flannel board story, felt, patterns given 1767:94-97
Little Red Riding Hood flannel board story, felt, patterns given 1767:132-136
Little Red Riding Hood; creative ideas and projects 1909:53-87
Rapunzel flannel board story, felt, patterns given 1767:143-149
The Fisherman and His Wife flannel board story, felt, patterns given 1767:154-158
The Frog Prince flannel board story, felt, patterns given 1767:150-153
The Musicians of Bremen Town flannel board story, felt, patterns given 1767:137-142
The Spindle, the Shuttle, and the Needle flannel board story, felt, patterns given 1767:112-115
GERMANY—FOLKLORE—HANDICRAFTS
Hansel and Gretel lunch bag gingerbread house, paper, colored glues, making 1763:29
Rumpelstiltskin story box theater, box, paints, ribbons, making 1763:44-45
Snow White and Rose Red talking bear, clothes-pin, paper, glue, making 1763:10-11
Snow White and the Seven Dwarfs seven sleepy dwarfs, egg cartons, pompoms, fabric, fiber-fill, making 1763:14-15
The Elves and the Shoemaker spool elves, spools, felt, eyes, cotton balls, making 1763:34-35
The Golden Goose sad and happy face princess, paper plate, yarn, paints, making 1763:30-31
GERMANY—FOLKLORE—PUPPETS
Little Red Riding Hood cup puppet, cups, yarn, ribbon, making 1763:24-25
Rapunzel in her tower puppet, paper tube, paints, yarn, making 1763:12-13
The Fisherman and his Wife fish in the ocean puppet, making 1763:38-39
The Frog Prince frog puppet, paper plates, colored paper, paints, party blower, making 1763:42-43
GERMANY—HANDICRAFTS
Beeswax modeling, beeswax, making 2054:83

Map making, paper, paints, making   2054:85
Pressed flowers, framed, paper, flowers, making
     2054:84

GHANA
Songs, stories, rhymes, puppets, crafts, patterns
     2231:105-116

GHANA—BIRTHDAYS—GAMES
Ampe game, how to play   1749:22-23

GHANA—CLOTH
Adinkira symbols printed on fabric, making
     1948:104-108
Adinkra cloth symbols on a goodbye card, mak-
     ing   1812:17-20
Block printing on white fabric, printing block,
     fabric ink, making   2200:22-23
Kente cloth, paper, crayons, making   1739:15-16

GHANA—CLOTHING
Ashanti printed cloth, painted T-shirt or handker-
     chief, making   2139:66
Adinkra cloth, quilt picture with symbols, how to
     do   1821:49
Kente, sandpaper printed cloth fabric, making
     2054:13

GHANA—COOKERY
Akwadu (baked bananas and coconuts), recipe
     1993:38
Sweet doughnut balls, recipe   2201:25

GHANA—CROWNS
Royal Ashanti gold crown and ring, pattern
     2231:114-115

GHANA—DOLLS
Akua-ba doll necklace, clay, pattern, making
     2212:120-121

GHANA—FLAGS
Fante people patchwork flags, how to copy tech-
     nique   1770:22-25

GHANA—FUNERALS
Lion coffin, boxes, pipe cleaners, wool, making
     1846:30

GHANA—GOLD
Gold weights used for balance scales, plasticine,
     paints, making   1739:19-20

GHANA—HANDICRAFTS
Ilukeres fly whisks, crepe paper, cardboard tube,
     making   2054:22

GHANA—NAMES
Children's names based on days of the week in
     Twi language   1749:23

GIACOMETTI, ALBERTO
Wire, clay and papier mache sculptures in
     Giacometti style, making   2049:24-25

GINGERBREAD
Basic kid-size gingerbread, recipe   2053:148
Ginger cake house, recipe   2225:88
Gingerbread cookies, recipe   2225:210
Gingerbread, recipe   2027:100
Gingerbread, recipe   2225:210

GOBLE, PAUL
Her Seven Brothers shadow puppet theater, story
     character patterns, how to do play   2060:39-48

GOD'S EYE
Eye of God, making   1875:181
Eye of God, sticks, yarn, making   2109:17
Ojo de Dios, God's eye, sticks, colored yarn,
     making   1750:87-88

GODZILLA. *See* **MONSTERS—COOKERY***

GOLD RUSH
Activities to celebrate Gold Rush Days   2175:16-20

GOLD RUSH—COOKERY
18-carat hash, recipe   2166:17
Blueberry-peach hand pies, recipe   2166:20
Campfire beefsteaks, recipe   2166:14
Chop suey, recipe   2166:27
Colache vegetable dish, recipe   2166:29
Hangtown fry, recipe   2166:23
Prospector's grub, bacon, beans, sardines, recipe
     1896:15
Sea biscuits, recipe   2166:11
Switchel beverage, recipe   2166:10

GOLDILOCKS AND THE THREE BEARS
Activities and projects to study theme of
     Goldilocks, patterns given   1927:1-64

GRANDPARENTS' DAY
Activities to celebrate   1791:211-215
Activities, crafts   1990:3-6
Activities, crafts   1991:3-6
Activities, crafts   1992:3-6
Science, language arts, art, music, math and social
     studies activities   2163:31-44

GRANDPARENTS' DAY—HANDICRAFTS
Family tree for gift, poster board, pattern for tree,
     making   2185:98-99

GREAT LAKES STATES
Activities and books   1918:67-76

GREECE
Songs, stories, rhymes, puppets, crafts, patterns
     2231:117-131

GREECE—CITIES
Walled city, boxes, cardboard, paints, making
     2054:88

GREECE—COINS
Bread dough coins, food coloring, dough, mak-
     ing   2054:86
Button coins, polymer clay, buttons, making
     2054:87

GREECE—COOKERY
Baklava pastry, recipe   2199:159
Baklava, honey soaked pastry dessert, recipe
     2222:119
Baklava, recipe   1920:160
Candy, amigthalo praline, recipe   2034:22
Eggs, scrambled, recipe   1776:26-27
Greek meat patties, recipe   2099:68-69
Greek spaghetti, recipe   1784:181

Hummus, recipe   1811:52-53
Koulourakia, sweet rolls, recipe   2174:30-31
Kouram bicthes, sugar cookies, recipe   1784:181
Lemon and egg soup, recipe   1933:20
Moussaka, recipe   2199:151
Navy bean soup, recipe   2199:68
Pomegranate dessert, recipe   2030:91
Spinach triangles, pastries, recipe   2222:116
Tzatziki dip, recipe   1863:26-27
White bean soup, recipe   2232:46-47
Yiahni, green beans and tomatoes, recipe   1784:182

GREECE—FESTIVALS—MASKS
Carnival; cricket mask, poster board, paints, making   2174:28-29

GREECE—GAMES
Hook the stick, how to play   1948:209

GREECE—WORRY BEADS
Worry beads, yarn, beads, making   1812:56-58

GREECE, ANCIENT—ARCHITECTURE
Columns, clay or cardboard tube column models, making   2139:153
Greek temple, card board cartons, paper, making   1951:66-67
Ionic column, matchbox, cardboard, making   2174:27
Parthenon; model of Parthenon, cardboard, paper towel tubes, making   1951:68
Temple column bookends, cardboard tubes, making   1835:14-15
Temple wall ornament, clay, cardboard, making   1997:88-91

GREECE, ANCIENT—ART
Underwater pictures about Alexander The Great inside his glass barrel, making   2048:8-9

GREECE, ANCIENT—ASTRONOMY
Zodiac cards, tag board, making   1835:28-29

GREECE, ANCIENT—BOATS
Miniature Greek boat model, cardboard, foil, making   1997:60-62

GREECE, ANCIENT—BREAD
History of bread   1950:27

GREECE, ANCIENT—CHARIOTS
Amphora jar prize, clay, paints, making   1997:52-55
Racing chariot model, can, boxes, cardboard, making   1997:48-51

GREECE, ANCIENT—CLOCKS
Clepsydra water clock, plastic bottles, making   1997:33-35

GREECE, ANCIENT—CLOTHING
Boy's chiton, old sheet, making   1997:9-11
Boy's himation, fabric, making   1997:12-13
Travel hat, red cardboard, making   1839:24-25

GREECE, ANCIENT—COINS
Design your own Greek coins, how to do   1997:40-41

GREECE, ANCIENT—COOKERY
Chicken dinner, recipe   1997:96-97
Cretan watercress salad, recipe   1857:9

Meze appetizer, recipe   1997:94-95
Pound cake with honey, recipe   1997:98-99
Yogurt, honey and nut dessert, recipe   1839:9

GREECE, ANCIENT—FESTIVALS—HANDICRAFTS
Festival of the Panathenaea; banner with owl decoration for goddess Athene, making   2187:28

GREECE, ANCIENT—FOOTWEAR
Sandals, leather, making   1857:13

GREECE, ANCIENT—FRESCOES
Dolphin fresco, plaster, paints, making   1835:10-11
Paint Minoan fresco, shoe box lid, plaster of Paris, making   1951:26

GREECE, ANCIENT—FRIEZE
Wall painting on paper, paints, making   2187:27

GREECE, ANCIENT—GAMES
Jackstones game, how to play   1940:38-39
Knucklebones, how to make and play   1976:6-7

GREECE, ANCIENT—HANDICRAFTS
Clay figures, clay, making   1976:12-13

GREECE, ANCIENT—JEWELRY
Earrings, beads, gold foil, gold cord, making   1997:81-83
Glass necklace, plasticine, plaster of Paris, clay, paints, making   1857:25
Golden charm bracelet, gold paint, gold beads, gold thread, making   1835:22-23
Greek chain jewelry, foil, glue, making   1857:19
Necklace of beads, beads, gold foil, gold cord, making   1997:78-80
Snake bracelet, wire, gold foil, making   1997:75-77

GREECE, ANCIENT—LABYRINTHS
Rolling ball maze, box with lid, marbles, making   1835:12-13

GREECE, ANCIENT—MEDICAL WORKERS
Caduceus model, making   1997:26-28

GREECE, ANCIENT—MODEL
Model of Ancient Greece, clay, rocks, making   1951:15-16

GREECE, ANCIENT—MUSICAL INSTRUMENTS
Monochord instrument, box, rubber bands, making   1951:75

GREECE, ANCIENT—MYTHOLOGY
Apollo and Daphne myth, river god picture, making   2048:13
Apollo and Daphne myth, Valentine day card, making   2048:12
Arachne, yarn webs, making   2139:157
Athena's owl, clay model, making   1997:6-9
Clay toy gift for the gods, clay, paints, making   2187:26
Daedalus and Icarus poster board wings, making   2139:156
Golden Fleece picture, making   2139:155
Great Earth Mother figure, making   1951:22
Hermes winged hat, cardboard, feather, making   2139:156

Medusa head, paper, cardboard, tissue paper, making 1976:22-23

Medusa mirror, papier mache, mirror, making 1835:32-33

Midas golden touch picture, gold paint, making 2139:157

Minotaur head, papier mache, making 1835:34-35

Minotaur's labyrinth maze, paper, yarn, making 2139:156

Pandora's box picture, making 2139:157

Peplos for goddess Athena, fabric, rope, making 1997:19-21

Poseidon's trident, cardboard, paints, making 1839:14

Poseidon's trident, shoe box lid, foil, making 1997:63-64

Trojan horse model, cardboard, craft sticks, making 1835:30-31

Trojan Horse picture, making 2139:155

Trojan horse treasure box model, shoe box, cereal box, cardboard, making 1997:35-38

Trojan horse; how to build horse on a wagon or table, making 1951:32-33

GREECE, ANCIENT—OLYMPIC GAMES

Fillets, armbands, and headbands, yarn, making 1857:43

Olympic plate, cardboard, making 1835:16-17

Olympic torch, black paper, colored tissue paper, making 1976:16-17

Olympic torch, cardboard, making 1839:18

GREECE, ANCIENT—POTTERY

Amphora model, clay, paints, making 2139:153

Hydria pot, clay, paints, making 1997:55-58

Painted vase, papier mache, making 1835:18-19

Red figure plate, clay, paints, making 1839:23

Terra-cotta horse, clay, making 1835:20-21

GREECE, ANCIENT—SIGNALS

Aeneas' signaling method, how to make and use 1857:41

GREECE, ANCIENT—SOLDIERS

Greaves bronze shin guards, poster board, making 1997:69-71

Helmet, paint bucket, paper, making 1997:66-69

Helmet, papier mache, making 1835:26-27

Hoplite's shield, cardboard, paints, making 1839:28-29

Shield with design, cardboard, markers, making 1997:71-73

Soldier's shield, cardboard, paints, making 2187:29

GREECE, ANCIENT—SPORTS

Clay vases with runner outlines, clay, gold pen, making 2050:9

Discus, paper plate, paints, making 1997:43

Silhouettes of athletes on paper vases, making 2050:9

Sportsmen scratchy pictures using wax crayon and paints, making 2050:8

Winner's crown, cardboard, ribbon, branches, making 1997:44-45

GREECE, ANCIENT—STATUES

Cycladic statues, foam board, tissue paper, making 1835:36-37

Statuette; plaster of Paris statuette, making 2139:152

GREECE, ANCIENT—THEATER MASKS

Actor's masks, paper plates, making 1997:30-32

Comedy and tragedy masks, making 1885:38-39

Greek theater mask, cardboard, making 1839:21

Greek tragedy mask, paper plate, clay, paint, making 2178:42-43

Papier mache comedy and tragedy mask, making 1951:91-92

Theater masks, cardboard, newspaper, paints, making 1976:18-19

Tragic and comic masks, clay, making 1835:24-25

GREECE, ANCIENT—THEATERS

Model of Greek theater from bakery box, making 1951:87-88

GREECE, ANCIENT—TOYS

Yo-yo, how to make ancient Crete yo-yo 1951:20

GREECE, ANCIENT—URNS

Athenian flower pot, how to paint 1951:83

GREECE, ANCIENT—VASES

Black-figure and red-figure vases, colored paper, making 1976:10-11

GREECE, ANCIENT—WEAVING

Loom to weave yarn into cloth, how to make and use 1997:15-18

Netting bag for collecting wool, making 1857:11

GREECE, ANCIENT—WRITING

How to write in Greek 1997:23-25

Wooden tablet with Greek writing, making 1976:4-5

GREENLAND—HANDICRAFTS

Scrimshaw, white plastic bottle, charcoal markers, making 2054:117

GROUNDHOG DAY

Activities to celebrate 1791:85-89

Activities, crafts 1990:47-50

Science, language arts, art, music, math and social studies activities 2163:183-196

GROUNDHOG DAY—COOKERY

Groundhog's zucchini bread, recipe 1790:7

GROUNDHOG DAY—DECORATIONS

Groundhog picture with hole and sun, paper, pattern, making 2207:36-37

GROUNDHOG DAY—PUPPETS

Groundhog shadow puppets, making 2163:185-188

Pop-up groundhog puppet, oatmeal box, yarn, felt, fiberfill, making 2153:42-43

GROUNDHOGS. See also WOODCHUCKS*

GUADELOUPE—COOKERY

Ratatouille Creole vegetable dish, recipe 1999:81

GUAM—WEAVING

Chamorro mat weaving, brown paper bags, tape, making 2054:143

H

HAIDA INDIANS—BUTTON BLANKETS
Button blanket crest sampler, felt, buttons, thread, making 2217:15-17
HAIDA INDIANS—TOTEM POLES
Stacking totem pole, cardboard containers, paints, making 1948:63-65
Totem pole with three raven beaks, tag board, coffee can, making 1762:52-57
HAITI—FESTIVALS—HANDICRAFTS
Carnival; lamayote, decorated small boxes with bug, mouse or lizard inside 1948:59-60
HAITI—HANDICRAFTS
Inner tube stamps, scrap wood, inner tubes, making 2054:118
Tin lid sculptures, tin cans, yarn, markers, making 2054:119
HALLOWEEN
Activities to celebrate 1791:40-45
Activities to celebrate 1993:11-14
Activities, crafts 1990:19-22
Activities, crafts 1991:19-22
Activities, crafts 1992:19-22
Activities, crafts 1994:11-14
Activities, literature, alternative holiday celebrations 1885:34-54
Science, language arts, art, music, math and social studies activities 2163:75-89
HALLOWEEN—COOKERY
Candy apples, recipe 2185:113
Caramel apples, recipe 2225:184
Caramel apples, recipe 2143:unp
Cider, recipe 1790:79
Eyeball cake, recipe 2225:185
Flaming eyes cake, recipe 2058:10
Jack-O-Lantern custard, recipe 2225:186
Jack-O-Lantern rice cakes, recipe 2058:9
Monster mash, recipe 2086:87
No-bake spider cookies, recipe 2086:86
Pumpkin bread, recipe 1784:182
Pumpkin cookies, recipe 1784:182
Pumpkin seeds, recipe 1784:183
Pumpkin shake, recipe 2225:187
Sand-witches, recipe 2058:8
Scary eyeball deviled eggs, recipe 2053:115
Seed snack, recipe 2143:unp
Swamp-water punch, recipe 2163:87
Wormy apples, recipe 2225:188

HALLOWEEN—DECORATIONS
3-D haunted house display, paper, making 2093:88
Animal mobile, cardboard, making 1828:29
Bat mobiles, paper, wire, making 2185:112
Cards and envelopes, making 1881:18-21
Cookie dough Jack-o-lantern, recipe 2085:24-25
Creepy crawly spider, paper, yarn, making 2143:unp
Doorstop pumpkin, brick, felt, making 2092:83
Haunted house treat box, milk carton, paper, yarn, making 2143:unp
Jack-o-lantern pin, bottle cap, felt, making 2092:83
Lantern from orange, making 1828:28
Pumpkin card, potato print, making 2128:74-75
Pumpkin cutouts, paper, making 1881:10-11
Real pumpkins, painted, paints, making 1881:14-15
Skull garland, large plastic bottle, string, pattern, making 2128:82-84
Spiders and webs, making 2163:77-84
Spiders, black pompom, pipe cleaners, making 1881:8-9
Treat bags, paper lunch bags, yarn, decorations, making 1881:16-17
HALLOWEEN—FACE PAINTING
Halloween face paints, recipe 1790:78
How to face paint 2143:unp
HALLOWEEN—FICTION
Funnybones by Janet Ahlberg; literature, activities, crafts 1898:4-9
Hubknuckles by Emily Herman; literature, activities, crafts 1898:10-15
Legend of Sleepy Hollow by Washington Irving; literature, activities, crafts 1898:28-33
Soup Bone by Tony Johnston; literature, activities, crafts 1898:16-21
Space Case by Edward Marshall; literature, activities, crafts 1898:22-28
HALLOWEEN—MASKS
Bird mask, paper plates, paper towel tube, pattern, making 2128:76-81
Paper bag masks, making 2143:unp
Paper plate and paper masks, making 1881:12-13
Shining skeleton, cardboard, glow in the dark paint, making 2178:24-25
Skeleton head stick mask, stick, poster board, paints, making 1766:27
Wicked witch, paper plate, paint, raffia, making 2178:22-23

HALLOWEEN—PATTERNS
Bat pattern   2226:7-8
Cat pattern   2226:9-10
Cornstalk, sheath of corn pattern   2226:11-12
Ghost pattern   2226:13-14
Jack-O-Lantern pattern   2226:15-16
Scarecrow pattern   2226:17-18

HALLOWEEN—PLAYS
Farmer Fred and the world's largest pumpkin
theater script   1806:63-73

HAND PUPPETS. *See* **PUPPETS—HAND***

HANUKKAH
Activities to celebrate   1993:27-30
Activities, crafts   1990:27-30
Activities, crafts   1991:27-30
Activities, crafts   1992:27-30
Activities, crafts   1994:27-30
Science, language arts, art, music, math and social
studies activities   2163:119-130
Story of Hanukkah   2023:2-47

HANUKKAH—COOKERY
Frosted fruit, recipe   2225:202
Latkes, recipe   1990:30
Latkes, recipe   1993:30
Latkes, recipe   1994:30
Latkes, recipe   1998:32
Latkes, recipe   2058:18
Latkes, recipe   2095:136
Latkes, recipe   2185:129
Lemon freeze, recipe   2225:203
Levivot or latkes, recipe   2177:15
Menorah sandwiches, recipe   2058:17
Mouse family's latke recipe   2115:last
Potato latkes, recipe   1784:187
Potato latkes, recipe   1790:91
Potato latkes, recipe   1847:28
Potato latkes, recipe   1920:78
Potato latkes, recipe   1920:80-81
Potato latkes, recipe   2023:27
Potato latkes, recipe   2133:29
Potato latkes, recipe   2201:219
Potato latkes, recipe   2225:204
Potato latkes, recipe   2233:5
Sesame-seed candy, recipe   2225:205
Spinning dreidels, recipe   2053:178
Star of David cookies, recipe   2225:206
Sufganiyyot, orange donuts, recipe   2185:132
Wassail drink, recipe   2201:220

HANUKKAH—DECORATIONS
Big dreidel, tissue boxes, cardboard tube, making
2154:58-59
Dreidel gift bag, paper shopping bag, paint, mak-
ing   2154:60-61
Dreidel pattern, making   2092:38
Dreidel, cardboard, pattern, making   2128:95-97
Dreidel, egg carton, toothpicks, making   1948:68-69

Dreidel, oak tag, dowel, pattern, making
2163:121-125
Hanukkiyah card, gold foil, pattern, making
2128:92-94
Happy Hannukah poster and dreidel chain, pattern,
making   2207:27-28
Menorah decoration, cardboard tube, paper cups,
foil, making   2154:56-57
Menorah from paper plates, paper, making
2090:106
Menorah from poster board, candles, making
2185:128
Menorah pattern, plastic wrap, foil, tag board,
making   2094:51-52
Menorah, juice cans, aluminum foil, paper towel
tubes, making   2128:98-100
Menorah, paper towel tubes, paper, making
2092:85
Menorah, paper, foil, markers, pattern given,
making   1948:37-38
Menorah, paper, patterns, making   2094:69
Menorah, thread spools, paints, making   2059:33
Menorah, woods, metal nuts, glitter, making
1790:90
Star of David stained glass window, paper, crayons,
making   2093:90
Window Star of David, plastic lids, yarn, tooth-
picks, making   2154:62

HANUKKAH—FICTION
Hershel and the Hanukkah Goblins by Eric Kimmel,
activities, crafts   2233:4-19

HANUKKAH—GAMES
Dreidel game, how to make and play   2185:130-131
Dreidel game, how to make and play   1847:29-32
Dreidel game, how to make and play   1990:28-29
Dreidel game, how to make and play   1992:28-30
Dreidel game, how to make and play   2011:15
Dreidel game, how to play   1948:70
Mouse children play game of dreidel   2115:last

HANUKKAH—PATTERNS
Candle pattern   2226:31-32
Dreidle pattern   2226:33-34
Menorah pattern   2226:35-36
Star of David pattern   2226:37-38

HARVEST FESTIVALS
Harvest superstitions   1936:33

HARVEST FESTIVALS—COOKERY
Bread, white, recipe   1936:31
Chinese moon cakes, recipe   2013:unp
Pongal dessert from India, recipe   2013:unp

HARVEST FESTIVALS—DOLLS
Corn doll, corn husks, string, cotton balls, making   1766:21

**HARVEST FESTIVALS—MUSICAL
INSTRUMENTS**
African harvest drum, tin can, balloons, tissue
paper, yarn, making   2013:unp

HATS

Bonnets, paper plate, decorative items, making 2055:193

HAWAII

Activities and books   1918:123-133

HAWAII—ANIMALS

Whales, 3-D whale picture, making   2139:219

HAWAII—BEACHES

Beaches, beach picture or colored sand in jar, making   2139:220

HAWAII—CLOTH

Tapa cloth, fabric design, patterns, making 1948:104-108

HAWAII—CLOTHING

Grass skirt, green paper, making   2139:215

HAWAII—COOKERY

Bread fruit donuts, recipe   1999:49

Hawaiian drumettes, recipe   1920:90

Luau chicken, recipe   2099:60-61

Macadamia coconut bread, recipe   1916:187

Macadamia nut biscuits, recipe   1930:75

Pineapple chicken kabobs, recipe   1859:169-170

Tropical fruit limpias with haupia sauce, recipe 2030:21

HAWAII—DANCES

Hula dancer, paper lunch bag hula dancer, making   2139:216

HAWAII—DECORATIONS

Pineapples, patterns, woven colored paper, making   2094:132

HAWAII—FISH

Tropical fish picture, making   2139:221

HAWAII—FOLKLORE

The Island-Below-The-Star by James Rumford, activities and recipes for the classroom 1916:183-187

HAWAII—KINGS

Feathered capes, butcher paper, making   2139:216

Royal standards (Kahili) staff, styrofoam cups, making   2139:216

HAWAII—LEIS

Aloha paper lei, adding machine tape, making 2054:146

Flower necklace, paper flowers, yarn, making 1948:115

Leis, tissue paper, making   2139:1217

Stitch-a-Lei, tissue paper, making   1785:102

HAWAII—LUAU PARTY—COOKERY

Banana bread, recipe   1783:76

Tropical twist drink, recipe   1783:76

HAWAII—MUSICAL INSTRUMENTS

Ukulese, cardboard, making   2139:216

HAWAII—NEW YEAR'S EVE—COOKERY

Dumpling soup, recipe   1790:98-99

HAWAII—NEW YEAR'S EVE— DECORATIONS

New Year's rockets, balloon, straw, making 1790:97

HAWAII—SHELLS

Shells, plaster of Paris shell casts, paints, making 2139:221

HAWAII—TREES

Palm tree pattern   2227:63

Palm trees, paper palm tree, making   2139:218

HAWAII—VOLCANOES

Volcano picture of magma model, making   2139:217

HEARTLAND STATES

Activities and books   1918:55-65

HEBREW LANGUAGE

Hebrew alphabet picture, making   2139:86

HERBS

Ancient herb garden, how to plant and care for 2073:110-115

Herbal bath powder, making   1973:39

Herbal home remedies   2073:118

Lavender wand, making   1973:38

HINDUS—FESTIVALS—COOKERY

Almond burfi dessert, recipe   2007:14

Holi; sweet milk dessert, coconut and almond, recipe   2031:29

HINDUS—FESTIVALS—JEWELRY

Raksha Bandham; rakhi bracelets, cardboard, buttons, ribbons, making   2007:14-15

HINDUS—FESTIVALS—LAMPS

Divali; lamps, paper, foil, glue, making   1739:62-63

HINDUS—FESTIVALS—MASKS

Divali Festival; Hanuman mask, cardboard, colored paper, long stick, making   2098:28

Holi; elephant mask, cardboard box, paints, making   2031:28

HINDUS—RANGOLI PATTERNS

Divali Festival; Rangoli patterns, black paper, white paper, paints, making   2098:29

HISPANIC AMERICANS. *See also* **MEXICAN AMERICANS; SPANISH AMERICANS**

HITTITES—CLOTHING

Hittite costume, fabric, making   1818:152

Shoes, socks, vinyl, making   1818:150-151

HITTITES—COOKERY

Hummus, recipe   1818:167

Lentil soup, recipe   1818:168

HITTITES—FOOD

Storing food in the ground, how to do   1818:166

HITTITES—JEWELRY

Pendant, gold foil, string, making   1818:153

HITTITES—MUSICAL INSTRUMENTS

Anatolian Sistrum, box, metal washers, making 1818:171-172

I

Raita condiment, recipe   2222:66
Raita yogurt dish, recipe   1987:21
Raita, recipe   1926:125
Raita,cucumber raita, recipe   1999:58
Rice pudding with cardamom, recipe   2222:70
Sooji, hot cereal dish, recipe   1825:102-103
Tandoori-style chicken, recipe   2222:68
Vegetable curry, recipe   2099:38-39
Yellow rice with potato and chickpeas, recipe
   2222:67
INDIA—FESTIVALS—COOKERY
Divali Festival; banana lassi drink, recipe   1987:29
Pongal Harvest Festival; Pongal rice, recipe
   2007:8
INDIA—FESTIVALS—HANDICRAFTS
Divali Festival; Alpanas good luck Hindu designs,
   making   2054:55
Divali Festival; divas lights, making   2007:26-27
Divali Festival; lamps, elephant, small bowl,
   self-hardening clay, making   1846:10
Divali Festival; lamps, paper, foil, glue, making
   1739:62-63
Divali Festival; rangoli patterns, making   2007:27
Dussehra Festival; large paper giant, making
   2139:37
Holi Festival; picture and painted T-shirt, making
   2139:38
Muharram Festival; tazia tomb model, craft
   sticks, tissue paper, making   2139:37-38
Raksha Bandhan; Brothers and Sisters Festival;
   bracelets, wool, beads, felt flowers, making
   1846:27
INDIA—FESTIVALS—MASKS
Divali Festival; Hanuman mask, cardboard, colored
   paper, long stick, making   2098:28
Pongal cow mask, poster board, pattern, making
   2231:146-147
INDIA—FESTIVALS—RANGOLI PATTERNS
Divali Festival; Rangoli patterns, black paper,
   white paper, paints, making   2098:29
Rangoli, Indian welcome message, making   1812:5-7
INDIA—FESTIVALS—SONGS
Eid-ul-Fitr Festival; Eid song   2007:29
INDIA—GAMES
Dice; make your own from clay, beads, bamboo
   canes   1870:6-7
Ganijifa cards; make from paper; how to play
   1870:20-21
Parchisi, make from fabric and clay, how to play
   1870:24-25
Spinning top, make from CD and knitting needle,
   how to play   1870:12-13
Tre-guti paper and pencil game, making
   1948:134-135
INDIA—HANDICRAFTS
Bas relief artwork, plaster of Paris, making   2139:39

Stone inlay, hobby gemstones, colored pebbles,
   clay, making   2054:57
**INDIA—HARVEST FESTIVALS—
   HANDICRAFTS**
Onam Harvest Festival; Pukalam (flower mat) by
   people of Kerala, fabric, wool, making   1846:19
INDIA—HOUSES
Courtyard with painted walls and floors, making
   2139:35
Mud huts, clay house, clay, paints, grass, making
   2139:35
INDIA—JEWELRY
Ankle bracelet, string, jingle bells, making
   1812:86-88
Bangles, beads, foil, making   2139:39
Bangles, wire, wool, gold thread, making   1871:21
Necklace of creatures, clay, beads, making
   1871:14-15
Rakhi bracelet, poster board, pattern, making
   2231:146-147
INDIA—LANGUAGE
A few Hindi words   1958:28
INDIA—MASKS
Elephant mask, paper, paint, sequins, making
   2139:45
INDIA—MOUNTAINS
Himalayas clay model, making   2139:42
INDIA—MUSICAL INSTRUMENTS
Twirling hand drum, wooden spoon, plastic tub,
   yarn, making   1948:152-153
INDIA—PAINTINGS
Religious paintings, paper, metallic gold paint,
   making   2139:39
INDIA—RAMAYANA SAGA
Princess Sita printed picture, poster paints, corks,
   making   2051:13
Ravana demon's ugly heads, paints, decorative
   materials, making   2051:12
INDIA—RIVERS
Ganges river mural, paper, markers, making
   2139:42-43
INDIA—THEATER
Face painting; Kathakali theater face painting,
   cold cream, paints, how to do   2054:56
Mask; Kathakali dance theater mask, gold foil,
   paper, pattern, making   2139:40
INDIA—TIE-DYE
Tie-dyeing, white cotton fabric, dyes, making
   2200:14-15
INDIA—TREES
Banyan tree picture, paper, yarn, glue, making
   2139:47
Mangrove trees picture, paper, paints, pattern,
   making   2139:47
INDIA—WEDDINGS—JEWELRY
Wedding wristband, ribbon, paper balls, making
   1871:19

Side-seam moccasins, leather or suede, making
    1931:84-86
INDIANS OF NORTH AMERICA—GAMES
Ball in the cup game, paper tube, yarn, making
    2110:30-31
Hand games, how to play   1948:164-165
Hul Gul hand game, how to play   1948:168
Pebble game, how to play   1952:78
Pebble game, how to play   2185:122
Ring and pin game, how to make and play
    1948:175
Rooster balance game, how to play   1952:78
Sierra Mewuk dice, walnuts, wax or clay, how to
    make and play   1934:87-88
Stick toss game, how to play   1992:9
Three stick toss game, how to play   1992:9
INDIANS OF NORTH AMERICA—GREAT PLAINS—CLOTHING
Buffalo-skin shirt, brown paper, white crepe paper,
    string, making   1977:10-11
INDIANS OF NORTH AMERICA—GREAT PLAINS—COOKERY
Corn cakes, recipe   1963:17
INDIANS OF NORTH AMERICA—GREAT PLAINS—DRUMS
Drum and drummer, cardboard box, paper, mak-
    ing   1977:22-23
INDIANS OF NORTH AMERICA—GREAT PLAINS—FOOTWEAR
Moccasins, fabric, thread, pattern, making
    1963:12-13
INDIANS OF NORTH AMERICA—GREAT PLAINS—HEADDRESSES
Warrior's headdress, paper, cardboard, feathers,
    making   1977:16-17
INDIANS OF NORTH AMERICA—GREAT PLAINS—MUSICAL INSTRUMENTS
Sun-dance drum, cardboard, fabric, felt, making
    1963:25
INDIANS OF NORTH AMERICA—GREAT PLAINS—PARFLECHES
Parfleche travel bag, paper, paints, string, making
    1963:22
INDIANS OF NORTH AMERICA—GREAT PLAINS—PICTOGRAPHS
Picture symbol stories, cardboard, paints, making
    1977:4-5
INDIANS OF NORTH AMERICA—GREAT PLAINS—PORCUPINE QUILLS
Porcupine weaving and braiding, straws, paints,
    making   1977:6-7
INDIANS OF NORTH AMERICA—GREAT PLAINS—POUCHES
Hunting pouch, fabric, thread, beads, making
    1963:15

INDIANS OF NORTH AMERICA—GREAT PLAINS—SHIELDS
Warrior's eagle shield, cardboard, fabric, felt,
    feathers, making   1963:19
Warrior's shield, cardboard box, feathers, mak-
    ing   1977:18-19
INDIANS OF NORTH AMERICA—GREAT PLAINS—SPIRITS
Whistle, cardboard, bamboo, clay, feather, mak-
    ing   1963:28
INDIANS OF NORTH AMERICA—GREAT PLAINS—TEEPEES
Tipi model, brown paper, straws, markers, mak-
    ing   1977:12-13
Tipi, fabric, 8 foot canes, sticks, making   1963:8-9
INDIANS OF NORTH AMERICA—HOUSES
Cattails or grass house, making   1931:66-67
Hogan home, making   1931:67-69
Teepee, full size, making   1931:69-76
Teepee, twigs, string, cloth, making   1807:15
INDIANS OF NORTH AMERICA—JEWELRY
Turquoise concho necklace or bolo ties, card-
    board, paint, making   2240:20-21
INDIANS OF NORTH AMERICA—MASKS
Eagle mask, buffalo mask, paper, patterns, mak-
    ing   1771:58-59
Styrofoam tray or cereal box mask, making
    2071:28-29
INDIANS OF NORTH AMERICA—MATS
Newspaper mat, how to weave   2071:30
INDIANS OF NORTH AMERICA—MUSICAL INSTRUMENTS
Indian drums, tin cans, making   2139:213
Leg rattles, bells, making   2139:213
Moraches rhythm sticks, making   1948:144
Stick rattle, stick, wire, yarn, colored beads,
    feathers, bells, making   2110:34-35
Tom-tom drum, tin can, making   1948:150-151
INDIANS OF NORTH AMERICA—PETROGLYPHS
Plaster of Paris petroglyphs, making   1739:145-147
INDIANS OF NORTH AMERICA—PUPPETS
Baby rattlesnake hand puppet, pattern, making
    2231:226-228
Brave warrior puppet, weather vane design, card-
    board, paints, patterns, making   1764:10-12
INDIANS OF NORTH AMERICA—ROPE
Making rope, how to do   1931:107-112
INDIANS OF NORTH AMERICA—SHIELDS
Paper plate shield, pattern, making   1948:92-95
INDIANS OF NORTH AMERICA—SOUTHWEST—JEWELRY
Turquoise and clay beads, beans, paints, making
    2110:22-23
INDIANS OF NORTH AMERICA—STORY BELTS
Story belts, oak tag, yarn, making   2093:89

IRELAND—FESTIVALS—COOKERY
Lammas Day; steak sandwich, recipe 2009:21
St. Patrick's Day; shamrock cookies, recipe
2103:30-31

IRELAND—FESTIVALS—HANDICRAFTS
Puck Fair; King Puck tweed goat, tweed fabric,
making 2009:26-27

IRELAND—FLAG
Pattern of flag 1948:42-43

IRELAND—FOLKLORE
Fin M'Coul, the Giant of Knockmany Hill by Tomie dePaola, activities, patterns 2159:41-52

IRELAND—GAMES
Cashlan Gherra board game, how to play
1948:136-137
Hit and span marble game, how to play 1948:172

IRELAND—HOUSES
Stone cottages, clay stone cottage model, making
2139:173

IRELAND—JEWELRY
Celt brooch, poster board, decorations, pattern,
making 2231:163-165

IRELAND—LACE MAKING
Irish lace, fabric lace copy, making 2139:175

IRELAND—LANGUAGE
Gaelic words for days of the week and numbers
2103:26
Greetings from Ireland in Irish 2009:7

**IRELAND—ST. PATRICK'S DAY—
DECORATIONS**
Leprechauns picture, paper plates, yarn, making
2139:176
Shamrock prints, sponges, green paint, pattern,
making 2139:176
Shamrock stencils, paper, paint, making 2054:90

IROQUOIS INDIANS—COOKERY
Succotash or Ogonsaganonda, recipe 1953:59
Succotash, recipe 1854:73

IROQUOIS INDIANS—DOLLS
Apple head dolls, making 1934:40-44
Corn dolls from corn husks, making 1934:32-35
Corn husk doll, corn husks, thread, making
1762:24-27
Corn husk doll, making 1864:28-29
Straw dolls and animals from natural materials,
how to make 1875:190-191

IROQUOIS INDIANS—FESTIVALS—GAMES
Green Corn Festival; beach stone game, how to
play 1936:26-27

IROQUOIS INDIANS—GAMES
Snow snakes, broomsticks, furniture wax, how to
make and play 2044:97-98

IROQUOIS INDIANS—GARDENING
More Sisters, sunflowers, beans and pumpkins,
how to grow 2073:126-132
Three Sisters of Life garden of corn, beans, and
squash, how to do 2073:120-125

IROQUOIS INDIANS—HOUSES
Longhouse, appliance box or shoe box longhouse, making 2139:205

IROQUOIS INDIANS—JEWELRY
Bean and seed necklace, making 2054:116

IROQUOIS INDIANS—MAPLE SYRUP
History of maple sugaring 2125:185-186
Legend of maple sugar 2125:182

IROQUOIS INDIANS—MASKS
False face paper mask, making 2139:209

IROQUOIS INDIANS—SCARECROWS
Zuni scarecrow, how to make 2073:131

IROQUOIS INDIANS—WAMPUM
Wampum, macaroni, food coloring, yarn, making
2078:22

IRVING, WASHINGTON
Legend of Sleepy Hollow; literature, activities,
crafts 1898:28-33

ISLAM
Multicultural Festival program, activities, art,
crafts, foods, folklore 1771:277-321

ISLAM—ART—HANDICRAFTS
Dome of the rock picture, gold paint, paper, making 2139:84

ISLAM—CALENDAR
Islamic lunar calendar research and art project,
making 1771:311-313

ISLAM—CARPETS
Design an Eastern rug, how to do 1771:291-292

ISLAM—COOKERY
Ayran or lassi, yogurt drink, recipe 1771:301-302
Lassi, yogurt based drink, recipe 1771:301-302
Moroccan pastry balls, recipe 1771:297-298
Muhammad's birthday cookies, recipe 1771:307-309
Tulumba tatlisi, sweet pastry, recipe 1771:299-300

ISLAM—FESTIVALS—DECORATIONS
Eid ul-Fitr; greeting card, paper, silver sparkles,
Islamic design given, making 1766:33

ISLAM—FESTIVALS—NOAH'S ARK
Feast of Ashura; Noah's Ark model and animals,
making 1771:303-306

ISLAM—FESTIVALS—NOAH'S ARK—COOKERY
Feast of Ashura; or Noah's Ark pudding, recipe
1771:306-307

ISLAM—MOSAICS
Mosaic canister, tin cans, paper, patterns, making
1771:285-286

ISRAEL
Judaism, Multicultural Festival program, activities,
art, crafts, foods, folklore 1771:363-382

ISRAEL—BIRTHDAYS—GAMES
Potato game, how to play 1749:28-29

ISRAEL—BIRTHDAYS—SONGS
Happy Birthday song to you in Hebrew 1749:46-47

ISRAEL—CARVINGS
Assyrian stone carvings picture, paper, paints,
making 2139:82-83

ISRAEL—CAVES
  Limestone caves, 3-D cave picture, puff paint, macaroni, making   2139:91
ISRAEL—COOKERY
  Challah, recipe   1811:25-29
  Chick peas with carrots, recipe   2011:21
  Matzo ball soup, recipe   1933:17
  Vegetable salad, recipe   2133:20
ISRAEL—DANCES
  Hora dance, how to do   2177:27
  Hora dance, how to do   2209:22
ISRAEL—DEAD SEA
  Dead sea picture, paper, salt, glue, making   2139:90
ISRAEL—DEAD SEA SCROLLS
  Dead sea scrolls, paper scrolls, cardboard tubes, making   2139:89
ISRAEL—FESTIVALS—HANDICRAFTS
  Menorah picture, black and yellow paper, making   2139:89
  Mezuzah, cardboard tubes, paints, making   2139:89
  Sukkot, toothpick shelters, leaves, glue, making   2139:90
ISRAEL—GAMES
  Dreydel game, how to make and play   1771:368-372
ISRAEL—HANDICRAFTS
  Havdallah candle picture, paper, making   2139:88
  Silver bells wind chimes, old silver ware, making   2054:60
  Spice box, small box, paint, spices, making   2139:88
  Stone mosaic, pebbles, tile, grout, making   2054:61
ISRAEL—JEWELRY
  Silver filigree jewelry, pie plate, making   2139:83
ISRAEL—LANGUAGE
  Greetings from Israel   2011:7
ISRAEL—MUSICAL INSTRUMENTS
  Lyre, cardboard, paint, string, making   2139:87
  Shofar, paper, tape, crayons, making   2139:87
  Tambourine, paper plate, yarn, bells, making   2139:87
ISRAEL—PILLARS
  Pillar of Absalom, clay pillar, small rocks, clay, making   2139:86
ISRAEL—SEALS
  Hebrew seals, clay disks, clay, toothpicks, paint, making   2139:83
ISRAEL—STAR OF DAVID
  Star of David festival display, cardboard, colored pens, making   1771:365-366
ISRAEL—WAILING WALL
  Wailing wall mural, paper, paints, dried grass, making   2139:85
ITALY
  Italy, Multicultural Festival program, activities, art, crafts, foods, folklore   1771:119-154

  Songs, stories, rhymes, puppets, crafts, patterns   2231:167-184
ITALY—ARCHITECTURE
  Marble portico, wall size, cardboard tubes, boxes, paints, making   1771:123-128
  Pisa, leaning tower model, tin cans, making   2139:139
ITALY—BEADS
  Trading beads, millefiori technique, plastic modeling material, making   1871:8-9
ITALY—BIRTHDAYS—SONGS
  Happy Birthday song to you in Italian   1749:46-47
ITALY—CHRISTMAS—COOKERY
  Eggplant and tuna salad, recipe   1901:28-29
  Old Befana's Italian almond macaroons, recipe   2233:22
  Sauteed shrimp, recipe   1901:27-28
  Spaghetti with clams, recipe   1901:25-26
ITALY—CHRISTMAS—FOLKLORE
  Legend of Old Befana by Tomie dePaola, activities, crafts   2233:21-26
ITALY—CHRISTMAS—HANDICRAFTS
  Nativity scene presepio, flour and salt dough, making   2012:9
ITALY—CITIES
  Pompeii, clay model, making   2139:140
  Venice mural, paper, paints, making   2139:140
ITALY—COOKERY
  Almond apricot biscotti cookies, recipe   2199:160
  Almond biscotti cookies, recipe   2222:82
  Bean and pasta soup, recipe   1926:62-63
  Bocconcini, cheese hors d'oeuvres, recipe   2199:142
  Bruschetta, toasted bread and vegetables, recipe   2222:76
  Calzone bread, recipe   2027:67-69
  Focaccia bread, recipe   2027:56-61
  Focaccia bread, recipe   2222:77
  Gnochi, potato dish, recipe   1920:83
  Lasagna, easy, recipe   2222:80
  Lemon granita cold dessert, recipe   1959:26-27
  Lemon granita, icy lemon dessert, recipe   2222:83
  Neapolitan pizza, recipe   2222:79
  Olive tree picture, making   2139:147
  Pasta picture, paper, glue, making   2139:147
  Pasta with spinach pesto, recipe   2222:81
  Pasta with tuna marinara sauce, recipe   2099:80-81
  Pizza, recipe   2027:62-66
  Pizzelle dessert, recipe   2199:163
  Polenta, cornmeal mush, recipe   2222:78
  Rice pie, recipe   1920:212-213
  Rigatoni, sweet, recipe   1743:28-29
  Spaghetti with oil and garlic, recipe   2201:264
  Turkey Bolognaise, recipe   1744:28-29
  Zucchini Toscano, recipe   1771:143-144
ITALY—EASTER—COOKERY
  Cassata ice cream, Sicilian, recipe   2129:29

ITALY—FESTIVALS—COOKERY

All Saints' Day; bean-shaped cookies, recipe 2129:17

Ferragosta (Virgin Mary Festival); mozzarella and tomato salad, recipe 2012:21

Saint Joseph's Day; fried cream puffs, recipe 1901:15-16

Saint Joseph's Day; rice and lentils, recipe 1901:17-18

Saint Joseph's Day; romaine salad with fennel, recipe 1901:18-19

ITALY—FESTIVALS—FLAGS

Palio horse race flags, fabric, wooden pole, paints, ribbon, making 2012:19

ITALY—FESTIVALS—MASKS

Carnival mask, cardboard, decorations, making 1812:78-81

Carnival; Venetian mask, cardboard, glasses, doily, crepe paper, making 2178:16

ITALY—FOLKLORE

Mysterious Giant of Barletta by Tomie de Paola, activities, patterns 2159:94-104

Strega Nona by Tomie de Paola, activities, patterns 2159:3-16

ITALY—GAMES

Bocce game, how to play 2247:22

Turbo, game for spinning top 1948:71

ITALY—GEOGRAPHY

Topographical map of Italy, making 2139:141

ITALY—HANDICRAFTS

Fancy eyeglasses, old frames, decorations, making 2054:91

Quill pen, feather, ink, making 2054:93

ITALY—HARVEST FESTIVALS—COOKERY

Olive Festival; spaghetti with garlic and olive oil, recipe 2012:27

ITALY—HISTORY

Italian Renaissance picture, making 2139:142

ITALY—HISTORY—BIOGRAPHY

Amerigo Vespucci early map, paper, markers, making 2139:145

Christopher Columbus's ships picture, making 2139:144

Galilei Galileo cardboard tube telescope, making 2139:145

Leonard da Vinci invention designs, making 2139:146

Marco Polo pictures of journeys, making 2139:146

ITALY—LANGUAGE

List of Italian words and phrases 1771:140-143

ITALY—LENT—COOKERY

Minestrone soup, recipe 2129:25

ITALY—MASKS

Paper pulp masks, making 1808:26

ITALY—MOSAICS

Ironed crayon mosaics, wax paper, crayons, making 2054:92

Medallions, Italian mosaic, mosaic patterns, making 2231:178,183

Mosaic picture, cardboard, paints, making 2140:18-19

Renaissance mosaic, paper model, colored papers, pattern, making 1771:128-132

ITALY—NEW YEAR'S EVE—COOKERY

Lentils and sausage dish, recipe 2129:21

ITALY—OPERA

Opera mural, butcher paper, paints, making 2139:143

ITALY—PAINTING

Baroque style of painting, make picture copy, making 2139:142

ITALY—PUPPETS

Pepitto marionette puppet, pattern, making 2231:177-182

Puppet theater cloth puppets, fabric, making 2139:143

ITALY—THEATER

Harlequinade theater, make picture, making 2139:144

IVORY COAST. *See also* **COTE D'IVOIRE**

IVORY COAST—HANDICRAFTS

Mud painting, embroidery hoop, muslin, making 2054:26

Printed fabric with symbols, patterns, making 1948:104-108

IVORY COAST—MUSICAL INSTRUMENTS

Drum, oatmeal box, paper, making 2054:27

J

JAMAICA—CHRISTMAS—COOKERY
Gingerbread, recipe   2015:9
JAMAICA—COOKERY
Coconut bread, recipe   1811:35-37
Jamaican beef turnovers, recipe   2222:20
Jerk chicken, recipe   2222:17
Pineapple fool dessert, recipe   1792:30-32
JAMAICA—FESTIVALS—COOKERY
National Heroes Day; tropical salad, recipe 2015:25
JAMAICA—FESTIVALS—COSTUMES
Jonkonnu Festival; Pitchy-Patchy man costume,
cardboard box, fabric, making   1792:28-29
JAMAICA—FESTIVALS—HEADDRESSES
Jonkonna Festival; headdress, cardboard, paints,
feathers, ribbons, making   2015:14-15
JAMAICA—GAMES
Dominoes game, how to make and play   1948:168
JAMAICA—HARVEST FESTIVALS—COOKERY
Harvest Sunday spinach salad, recipe   2015:23
JAMAICA—MUSIC
Maracas, plastic bottles, dried beans, making 1792:26
JAMAICA—WEAVING
Weave a fish, paper, paints, making   2015:20-21
JAPAN
Activities, literature, family history   1885:55-90
Japan, Multicultural Festival program, activities,
art, crafts, foods, folklore   1771:155-191
JAPAN—CATS
Lucky cat money box, clay or papier mache,
making   1807:19
JAPAN—CLOTHING
Kimono, man's dress shirt, scarves, making 2139:21
JAPAN—COOKERY
Chicken kebabs, recipe   2222:89
Fruit kebabs with plum sauce, recipe   2222:94
Ginger pork chops, recipe   2222:91
Gohan (rice), recipe   2016:27
Kappa Maki (cucumber rolls), recipe   2201:72
Kushiyaki, recipe   1811:61-64
Kyushu vegetable rice, recipe   2222:90
Parent and child rice bowl, rice, egg, chicken,
recipe   2222:93
Rice and bean paste balls, recipe   2222:95
Rolled sushi, recipe   2222:88
Sushi rice, recipe   2201:71
Sushi, recipe   1926:156-158
Teriyaki chicken wings, recipe   2099:28-29
Vegetable tempura, recipe   2222:92
Yakitori, chicken kabobs, recipe   1926:186-187

JAPAN—DANCES
Sakura song and ribbon dance   1885:59-60
JAPAN—DOLLS
Daruma doll, clay, paints, making   2016:11
Daruma doll, plastic egg, clay, making   2139:29
Daruma doll, plastic eggs, paints, making   2108:16-17
Kimono doll, stiff white and colored paper, origami
paper, making   2016:29
Origami doll, making   2108:75
JAPAN—FANS
Accordion fan, round or oval fan, sliding fan,
how to make   1771:160-163
Craft sticks and paper fan, making   1875:162-163
JAPAN—FESTIVALS—COOKERY
Obon Buddhist Festival; cold savory custards,
recipe   1908:29
Setsubun Festival; miso-topped bean curd, recipe
1908:21
Shichi-Go-San Girls Festival; orange baskets,
recipe   1908:25
Shrine Festival; orange baskets, recipe   2016:23
JAPAN—FESTIVALS—DOLLS
Shichi-Go-San Festival; kimono doll, stiff white
and colored paper, origami paper, making
2016:29
JAPAN—FESTIVALS—HANDICRAFTS
Boy's Festival; carp kites, cloth, wire, making 1846:26
Koi Festival; Koi, paper lunch bag carp, making
2139:29
New Year; fans, paper, popsicle sticks, making
1846:11
Sapporo Snow Festival; snow sculpture, making
1948:200
Star Festival (Tanabata Matsuri); banner, paper,
yarn, making   2139:30
Star Festival; tanabata, paper, crayons, pattern
given, making   1948:39-41
Tokonoma Festival; build a corner of beauty with
Kakemono, hanging scroll, how to make
1771:156-160
JAPAN—FESTIVALS—KITES
Children's Day Festival; carp kite, paper, paints,
string, making   1771:166-168
JAPAN—FESTIVALS—LANTERNS
Star Festival (Tanabata); temple light, boxes,
paints, candles, patterns, making   1771:173-175
JAPAN—FESTIVALS—ORIGAMI
Star Festival (Tanabata Matsuri); origami decora-
tion, making   2241:20-21

50

Frog, boat and swan paper-folded origami, how
to do   1875:166-167
Hat from origami paper, making   1960:26-27
Hop toad, origami paper, making   1948:5
House, animal and puppet, origami paper, patterns,
making   1771:170-173
Paper popper, origami paper, making   1948:7
Rocking bird, origami paper, making   1948:3
Square, origami paper, making   1948:2

JAPAN—PAPER
Marbled paper, paper, oil, paints, making   1808:14
Paper pulp pictures, making   1808:19

JAPAN—POTTERY
Clay bowl, clay, paints, making   2139:23
Clay slab dish, making   2108:22-23

JAPAN—PUPPETS
Banraku tag board puppet, making   2139:26
Japanese stick puppets, making   2108:30-31

JAPAN—SAMURAI
Samurai armor, making   2108:26-27
Samurai helmet, newspaper for full-size and origami
paper for model helmets, making   2016:21
Samurai warriors, armor helmet, sword, paper,
foil, making   2139:27

JAPAN—SERVING TABLE
Serving table to serve food, wood, making   1952:160

JAPAN—SPRING
Easy butterfly net, making   1948:193-194

JAPAN—TEA CEREMONY
Tea ceremony, how to do   1739:58-59

JAPAN—THEATER—MASKS
Japanese theater mask, Noh mask, cardboard,
paints, making   2178:60-61
No Theater masks, paper plates, making   2139:26
Noh play masks, paper plates, paints, patterns,
making   1771:178-179
Old man No mask, pattern, making   2108:77
Two No masks, Saru, monkey mask, making
2108:24-25

JAPAN—TIE-DYE
Tie-dyeing, white cotton fabric, dyes, making
2200:14-15

JAPAN—TOYS
Welcoming cat, making   2108:76

JAPAN, ANCIENT—ARTISTS
Hokusai wood cuts of mountains and Mount Fuji
volcano, plasticine, making   2047:8-9

JAVA. *See also* **INDONESIA**

JAVA—BATIK
Batik design on old sheet, candle, paints, making
2140:26-27
Batik tulis, written batik, fabric, food coloring,
making   2054:67-68

JESUS CHRIST. *See also* **BIBLE—HANDICRAFTS;**
CHRISTIANITY; NATIVITY

JEWELRY. *See also* **BEADS**

JEWISH COOKERY
Almond roca, recipe   1902:18-19
Challah braid, recipe   1950:25-26
Challah bread, recipe   1784:186
Cheese latkes, recipe   1784:186
Cheese latkes, recipe   1920:157
Hamburgers, recipe   1902:20-21
Kreplak, Jewish wontons, recipe   1920:111
Latkes, recipe   1926:140-141
Noodle kugel, recipe   1920:159
Potato knishes, recipe   1902:15-17
Seder charoseth paste, recipe   2133:17
Sweet noodle kugel, recipe   1920:157

JEWISH SABBATH. *See also* **SABBATH**

JEWISH SABBATH—COOKERY
Challah bread, recipe   1853:unp
Challah bread, recipe   1934:89-92
Challah, recipe   2027:122-124

JEWISH SABBATH—HANDICRAFTS
Challah bread cover, yarn, napkins, making   1853:unp

JEWS—FOLKLORE
It Could Always be Worse story with whole language activities   1768:15-19

JOAN OF ARC
Activities from easy to difficult to study her life
2022:3-46

JOHNNY APPLESEED. *See also* **APPLES;**
CHAPMAN, JOHN
Activities to celebrate Johnny Appleseed Day
1791:105-109
Theater script   1806:11-16

JOHNNY APPLESEED—BIRTHDAY
Activities, crafts   1990:7-10
Activities, crafts   1991:7-10

JOHNNY APPLESEED—COOKERY
Applesauce, recipe   1990:10
Caramel apples, recipe   1990:10
Johnny Appleseed cake, recipe   2225:90
Waldorf apple salad, recipe   1806:16

JOHNNY APPLESEED—DECORATIONS
Headband with apple cutout, making   2089:264

JOHNNY APPLESEED—GAMES
Johnny goes a planting game, how to play   2088:142

JOHNNY APPLESEED—HATS
Paper hat with apple cutout, making   2088:142

JOURNALS
Pamphlet bound notebook in a polaire, making
1868:44-46
Travel journal that unfolds, making   1868:57-59

JUDAISM
Judaism, Multicultural Festival program, activities,
art, crafts, foods, folklore   1771:363-382

JUDAISM—STAR OF DAVID
Star of David festival display, cardboard, colored
pens, making   1771:365-366

JUMPING JACKS. *See also* **PANTINS—FRANCE***

JUNK FOOD. *See* **FOOD—JUNK FOOD***

K

KACHINA DOLLS
Kachina dolls, cardboard tubes, papier mache, paints, fabric, feathers, making 1771:54
KACHINA DOLLS. *See also* **HOPI INDIANS**
KANSAS
Activities and books 1918:55-65
KANSAS—COOKERY
Grilled Swiss cheeseburger with mushrooms, recipe 1859:100
KANSAS CITY—COOKERY
Curried chocolate and sweet potato soup, recipe 1933:47
KELLER, HELEN
Activities from easy to difficult to study her life 2021:2-47
KENTUCKY
Activities and books 1918:99-109
KENTUCKY—COOKERY
Hot brown sandwich, recipe 1794:65
Kentucky burgoo stew, recipe 1859:65-66
Kentucky derby pie, recipe 2193:121
KENYA—BEADWORK
Beaded ornaments, beads, wire, thread, making 2136:13-15
KENYA—CHRISTMAS—COOKERY
Simsim cookies, recipe 2032:19
KENYA—CLOTH
Kente cloth, paper, crayons, making 1739:15-16
KENYA—COOKERY
Kenyan crunch bananas, recipe 2222:10
Peanut soup, recipe 1916:165
Vermicelli and raisins, recipe 2002:51
KENYA—FESTIVALS—COOKERY
Id-ul-Fitr; kaimati, sugar coated doughnut, recipe 2032:23
KENYA—FOLKLORE
Elephants for Kids by Anthony D. Fredericks, activities and recipes for the classroom 1916:163-165
KENYA—GAMES
Jacks, make from clay or pebbles, how to play 1870:10-11
Mancala board, make from egg cartons and tissue paper, how to play 1870:22-23
KENYA—SYMBOLS
Tiny carved drum symbol, dowel, leather, beads, making 1871:25

KENYA—THANKSGIVING—COOKERY
Spiay corn, recipe 2032:29
KENYA—WEDDINGS—COOKERY
Tropical fruit punch, recipe 2032:27
KING, MARTIN LUTHER, JR.
Activities to celebrate 1993:39-42
Activities, crafts 1990:39-42
Activities, crafts 1991:39-42
Activities, crafts 1992:39-42
Activities, crafts 1994:39-42
Freedom garden, how to prepare and plant 1790:2
KING, MARTIN LUTHER, JR.—BIRTHDAY
Activities to celebrate 1791:80-84
KING, MARTIN LUTHER, JR.—COOKERY
Raspberry and orange sherbet punch, recipe 1790:3
KING, MARTIN LUTHER, JR.—DECORATIONS
Banner, felt, yarn, cardboard, making 2153:32-33
Peace train bulletin board with peaceful thought on each train, making 2090:294
Peace wreath, paper, ribbons, making 2185:25
KING, MARTIN LUTHER, JR.—FICTION
Martin Luther King Day by Linda Lowery, activities, crafts 2233:38-43
KING, MARTIN LUTHER, JR.—JEWELRY
Friendship bracelet, beads, yarn, making 2185:24
Necklace with picture, craft sticks, ribbon, pattern, making 2207:33
KING, MARTIN LUTHER, JR.—PATTERNS
Hand pattern 2226:73-74
World pattern 2226:75-76
KING TUT. *See* **EGYPT—ANCIENT***
KIRGHIZ NOMADS—FELT
Felt balls, jewelry, wall hangings, figures, fleece, carded wool, knitted wool, making 2200:10-11
KITES
March lion kite, tag board, streamers, string, making 2087:60-61
KLIMT, GUSTAV
Klimt mosaic of marble inlaid with gold, trees and flowers, making 2047:12-13
KNIGHTS—HELMETS
Knight's helmet and sword, cardboard, duct tape, aluminum foil, making 1954:55
KNIGHTS—TABLES
Round table, making 1861:35
KNIGHTS—WEAPONS
Sword hilt, plasticine, clay, paint, making 1861:25
KOREA, SOUTH. *See also* **SOUTH KOREA**

KOREA—BIRTHDAYS—SONGS

Happy Birthday song to you in Korean   1749:46-47

KOREA—BUDDHA'S BIRTHDAY—COOKERY

Pajon, omelet like dish, with dipping sauce, recipe   2056:13

KOREA—BUDDHA'S BIRTHDAY—LANTERNS

Lantern, paper, watercolor paints, embroidery thread, making   2056:15

KOREA—COOKERY

Korean dumplings, recipe   1920:106

KOREA—FESTIVALS—HANDICRAFTS

Alphabet day; beautiful letter, making   1948:127

Tano or Double Five Festival; fan, paper, craft sticks, watercolor paints, embroidery thread, making   2056:19

KOREA—HANDICRAFTS

Jeweled crown, heavy paper, decorations, making   2054:69

Pajagi, sheer wrapping cloth, making   2108:42-43

KOREA—HARVEST FESTIVALS—COOKERY

Chusok or Harvest Moon Festival or Korean Thanksgiving; kimchi (pickled cabbage dish), recipe   2056:21

KOREA—LANTERNS

Lantern; plastic lid lantern, pattern given, making   1948:32-33

Paper lantern, paper, tape, pattern given, making   1948:30-31

Paper lanterns, paper, yarn, glitter, making   1812:95-97

KOSSOF, LEON

Water world pictures in Kossof style of swimmers, divers and waves, making   2050:28-29

KUNA INDIANS—MOLAS

Mola patch, fabric, paper, embroidery thread, making   1913:31

KWANZAA

Activities to celebrate   1791:69-74

Activities to celebrate   1993:35-38

Activities, crafts   1990:35-38

Activities, crafts   1991:35-38

Activities, crafts   1992:35-38

Activities, crafts   1994:35-38

Science, language arts, art, music, math and social studies activities   2163:151-169

KWANZAA—COOKERY

Akwadu (baked bananas and coconuts), recipe   1993:38

Baked sweet potatoes or yams, recipe   1790:96

Benne sesame seed cakes, recipe   2228:unp

Flag cookies, recipe   2058:24

Peanut stew, recipe   2185:146

Stuffed bananas, recipe   2058:23

KWANZAA—DECORATIONS

Bell bracelet, pipe cleaners, bells, making   1790:95

Candles, making for Kwanzaa   2163:153-161

Corn magnet, cereal box, tissue paper, bubble wrap, making   2153:22-23

Helping hands coupon booklets to give to family, making   2090:293

Kinara candle holder, jars, tissue paper, ribbon, making   2128:122-123

Kinara candle holder, paper, pattern given, making   1948:34-36

Kinara candles in holder, wood, nails, paints, making   2185:148

Kinara from paper, clothespins, paper, making   2090:107

Mazao bowl, plastic bowl, papier mache, paints, making   2185:147

Mekela straw mat, making   1791:72

Mkeka mat, paper, crayons, making   2092:87

Mkeka place mat, paper, paints, making   2059:45

Mkeka; weaving paper place mats, making   1948:22-23

Place mats, black, red and green paper, making   2128:124-126

Ribbon card, old card, ribbon, making   2128:118-121

Vibunzi, ears of corn, paper, making   2059:47

We celebrate Kwanzaa poster, pattern, making   2207:29

KWANZAA—HANDICRAFTS

Cow tail switch, paper roll, fabric, decorations, making   2228:unp

Dashiki design African shirt, paper model, making   1993:36-37

L

M

Tacos and taco sauce, recipe 1926:80-81

Tacos, tortillas, filled with vegetables, beans, cheese, meat, recipe 2035:28-29

Tomato pumpkin seed salsa, recipe 2222:100

Tortillas, recipe 1750:71-72

Tortillas, recipe 2114:23

Tostadas, recipe 2099:90-91

MEXICO—EASTER—COOKERY

Lentil soup, recipe 2005:21

MEXICO—EASTER—HANDICRAFTS

Easter cascarones, eggshells, colored tissue papers, decorations, making 1762:34-39

Easter cascarones, painted eggshells, making 2139:197

MEXICO—FESTIVALS

Feast of the Radishes; activities to celebrate 2175:88-91

MEXICO—FESTIVALS—COOKERY

Celebration cookies, recipe 2222:107

Cinco de Mayo; menudo hearty soup, recipe 2114:74

Cinco de Mayo; sopaipillas bread, recipe 2185:66

Day of the Dead; chocolate soda, recipe 1790:83

Day of the Dead; hot chocolate, recipe 2111:14

Day of the Dead; Pan de Los Muertos bread, recipe 1920:17

Day of the Dead; salsa cruda sauce, recipe 2005:25

MEXICO—FESTIVALS—GOD'S EYE

Feast of the Ripe Fruits; God's eye, craft sticks, colored yarn, making 2111:29

God's eye, sticks, colored yarn, making 1750:87-88

MEXICO—FESTIVALS—HANDICRAFTS

Cascarones; confetti filled egg cones, making 2109:69

Cinco de Mayo; fiesta place mats, paper, making 2059:95

Cinco de Mayo; hanging horse pattern, making 2205:38

Cinco de Mayo; yarn art, cardboard, yarn, making 2059:94

Day of the Dead, El Dia del Muerte; paper skeleton, making 2139:196

Day of the Dead; candy skull, making 2114:87

Day of the Dead; gravestone rubbings, making 1790:82

Day of the Dead; paper marigold bouquet, crepe paper, pipe cleaners, making 2114:88

Day of the Dead; skeleton, modeling clay, tin can, wire ring, making 1871:16-17

Day of the Dead; sugar skulls, icing, cake decorations, candies, making 1846:30

Day of the Dead; tree of life candlestick, clay birds, flowers, leaves, making 1846:31

Day of the Dead; wire animals and birds, making 1808:27

Feast of the Radishes; radish sculpture, making 2175:89

Feast of the Radishes; Yucatan bird trivet, ceramic tile, pattern, making 2175:91-92

Papel picado pierced paper banner, tissue paper, making 2114:28-29

Paper cuts decorations, tissue paper, string, making 2109:73

Tissue paper flowers, making 2139:197

MEXICO—FESTIVALS—MUSICAL INSTRUMENTS

Cinco de Mayo; maracas, papier mache, making 2185:67

MEXICO—FESTIVALS—PINATAS

Cinco de Mayo; individual pinatas, lunch bags, ribbon, candies, making 2059:96

MEXICO—FESTIVALS—PUPPETS

Day of the Dead; dancing skeleton puppet, papier mache, springs, paints, making 1764:20-22

Day of the Dead; skeleton puppets, cardboard, sticks, string, making 2111:13

MEXICO—FESTIVALS—TIN WORK

Cinco de Mayo; Mexican tin ware, cardboard, foil, making 2059:93

MEXICO—FOLKLORE

Snake Loses his Dinner story with whole language activities 1768:47-55

MEXICO—GAMES

Batero game, how to make and play 2109:69

Bottle cap tower, how to make and play 1948:174

Dice; make your own from clay, beads, bamboo canes, how to play 1870:6-7

La Loteria; picture lotto, make from cardboard, how to play 1870:18-19

The ribbons, los histones game, how to play 2114:12

Tlachtli ball game, how to play 2114:47

MEXICO—GOD'S EYE

Ojo de Dios, yarn, making 2114:14

Ojo de Dios, yarn, making 2139:202

Ojo de Dios, yarn, sticks, making 1948:101-103

MEXICO—HANDICRAFTS

Butterflies marble painted, plastic bag or inkblot butterflies, making 2139:199

Clay sun faces, clay, paints, making 2054:121

Festive flag paper cut-outs, colored paper, making 1808:11

Glider, paper glider, making 1948:11

Mexican flowers, tissue paper, making 2094:102

Poinsettia, picture of paper poinsettia, making 2139:200

MEXICO—HATS

Sombrero, cardboard sombrero, making 2139:195

MEXICO—LANGUAGE

Words and everyday phrases in Spanish 2114:10-11

MEXICO—MURALS

Murals, butcher paper Mexican mural, making 2139:201

MEXICO—MUSICAL INSTRUMENTS
Maracas from paper plates and dried beans or rice, making 2141:7
Maracas, papier mache, making 2139:197

MEXICO—NEW YEAR'S DAY—COOKERY
Rosco de Reyes, New Year's bread, recipe 1950:82-83

MEXICO—OLMEC PEOPLE
Olmec stone head model, paper, markers, making 2139:191
Olmec style stone head model, plaster of Paris, making 2114:37

MEXICO—PINATAS
Ballon and papier mache pinata, making 2114:17-18
Donkey paper sack pinata, pattern, making 2231:195-197
Fiesta pinata, papier mache, paints, balloon, making 2054:123
Paper bag pinata, making 2141:7
Papier mache over balloon decorated pinata, making 2035:30
Papier mache pinata, making 1766:11
Papier mache pinata, tissue paper, making 2161:156-157
Personal pinatas for group of children, balloons, papier mache, candies, making 2090:298
Pinata from papier mache covered balloon, making 1934:70-73

MEXICO—POTTERY
Pottery, clay or papier mache pot, making 2139:201-202

MEXICO—PUPPETS
The Coyote Scolds his Tail puppet show, pattern for coyote 2231:188-192

MEXICO—PYRAMIDS
Build a Maya step pyramid, how to do 2114:46

MEXICO—RAIN STICKS
Rain stick, paper tube, cylinder can, nails, making 2141:49

MEXICO—RELIGION—HANDICRAFTS
Metepec Tree of Life, bakers clay, pattern, making 2109:63
Milagro miracle decoration, aluminum foil, making 2114:84
Tree of Life candleholder, clay, paints, making 2114:81-83

MEXICO—TIN WORK
Aluminum ornaments, aluminum, paints, yarn, making 1913:13-15
Framed tin plate, tin plate, hammer, nails, making 2054:124
Ornaments, aluminum foil, cardboard, making 1934:68-69

MEXICO—TOLTEC INDIANS
Toltec columns, refrigerator box, making 2139:192

MEXICO—TOYS
Bottle cap tops, plastic caps, toothpicks, making 1948:66

MEXICO—WEAVING
Wall hanging on cardboard loom, yarn, how to do 2139:10-11

MEXICO—WEDDINGS—COOKERY
Wedding cookies, pecans, butter, recipe 2005:17

MEXICO—WOODEN ANIMALS
Wooden animals, sticks, twigs, paints, making 1807:18

MICHIGAN
Activities and books 1918:67-76

MICHIGAN—COOKERY
Blueberry muffins, recipe 1817:66
Cherry pie, recipe 1983:97
Ice cream with cherry sauce in a tortilla shell, recipe 1859:103
Molasses sugar cookies, recipe 1920:183

MIDDLE AGES—BOOKS
Book of Days, how to make and bind 1954:78-79
Illuminated letter, paper, paints, making 1841:23

MIDDLE AGES—CASTLES
Cardboard or wood castle with moat and drawbridge, making 1954:44-45

MIDDLE AGES—CATAPULT
Catapult from cardboard and elastic bands, making 1954:47

MIDDLE AGES—CHURCHES
Gargoyle, cardboard, clay, making 1841:27

MIDDLE AGES—CLOCKS
Hour glass sand clock, bottles, sand, making 1954:10

MIDDLE AGES—CLOTHING
Boy's tunic, sheet, scarf, tights, making 1740:26
Girl's dress or kirtle, sheet, scarf, tights, making 1740:26
Purse, felt, making 1841:28

MIDDLE AGES—COAT OF ARMS
Coat of arms, cardboard, paints, tape, making 1740:28

MIDDLE AGES—COOKERY
Bread bowls for soup, how to make 1950:38
Honey toast, recipe 1841:18-19
Peas pottage, green peas, milk, recipe 2135:33
Rose petal bread, recipe 1954:39-40

MIDDLE AGES—FESTIVALS
Midsummer's Eve chant and secret meaning of chant 1954:71

MIDDLE AGES—FOUR ALLS
Four alls diorama model of medieval society, making 1954:26-29

MIDDLE AGES—GAMES
Bob for apples game, how to play 1954:69
Bocci ball, how to play 19545:70
Capture the flag, how to play 1954:53

Hunt the slipper game, how to play   1954:32
Oranges and lemons game, how to play   1954:70

MIDDLE AGES—HERBS
Grow a medieval drugstore of herbs, how to do
    1954:83
Herb garden, how to plant   2135:19

MIDDLE AGES—JEWELRY
Brooch, cardboard, clay, making   1841:16-17
Chain, paper, foil, glue, making   1740:27
Rose petal necklace, making   1954:65

MIDDLE AGES—KNIGHTS
Knight's helmet and sword, cardboard, duct tape,
    aluminum foil, making   1954:55
Shield, cardboard, paints, making   1841:15

MIDDLE AGES—MANUSCRIPTS
Illuminated manuscript, paper, colored pencils,
    making   1740:29

MIDDLE AGES—PILGRIMS
Pilgrim's scallop badge, clay, paint, glue, making
    1740:28

MIDDLE AGES—PLAYS
St. George and the dragon play, how to perform
    1954:72-73

MIDDLE AGES—STAINED GLASS
Stained glass window, tissue paper, making   1841:24

MIDDLE AGES—TOYS
Juggling balls, fabric, rice, making   1841:20
Toy soldier, cardboard, paints, making   1841:7

MIDDLE AGES—WASSAILING
Wassail a fruit tree, how to do   1954:69

MIDDLE AGES—WEAVING
Tapestry, how to weave your own, cardboard,
    wool, yarn, making   2135:29

MIDDLE ATLANTIC STATES. *See also*
    **DELAWARE; MARYLAND; NEW
    JERSEY; PENNSYLVANIA**
Activities and books   1918:87-97

MIDDLE ATLANTIC STATES—COOKERY
Delaware snow cream, recipe   1789:108
Dutch apple meringue, recipe   1789:108
Dutch shoo-fly pie, recipe   1789:104
Funnel cakes, recipe   1789:106
Hot potato salad, recipe   1789:102
Jewish rye bread, recipe   1789:99
Maryland crab cakes, recipe   1789:102
Maryland fried oysters, recipe   1789:101
Matzo ball soup, recipe   1789:101
Minehaha cake, recipe   1789:107
New York cheesecake, recipe   1789:105
Snickerdoodles, recipe   1789:103
Soft pretzels, recipe   1789:100
South Philly cheese steak sandwiches, recipe
    1789:103

MIDDLE EAST. *See also* **ARABIAN PENINSULA***
MIDDLE EAST—COOKERY
Baba ganouche, eggplant dish, recipe   1999:40

Dried fruit salad with orange juice, recipe
    2138:28-29
Hummus, recipe   1926:106-107
Lamb shish kebabs, recipe   2222:117
Pita bread, recipe   1950:10
Pita, pocket bread, recipe   2027:70-72
Rice and lentil salad, recipe   2222:114
Roasted eggplant dip, recipe   2222:112
Sesame seed twists, recipe   2222:118
Stuffed grape leaves, recipe   2099:40-41
Stuffed grape leaves, recipe   2222:113
Stuffed peppers, recipe   2222:115
Tabbouleh, recipe   1926:174-175

MIDDLE EAST—FESTIVALS—COOKERY
Id pudding, vermicelli, butter, sugar, raisin,
    almonds, recipe   2042:28

**MIDDLE EAST—FESTIVALS—GREETING
    CARDS**
Id card with Arabic writing, cardboard, making
    2042:29

MIDSUMMER EVE
Midsummer's Eve chant and secret meaning of
    chant   1954:71

MIDWEST—COOKERY
Angel food cake, recipe   1789:136
Cherry pie, recipe   1789:138
Chicago deep-dish pizza, recipe   1789:133
Cinnamon rolls, recipe   1789:131
Coffeecake, recipe   1789:132
Coneys, recipe   1789:135
Dutch apple kuchen, recipe   1789:137
Fish balls, recipe   1789:135
Pasties, recipe   1789:134
Spritz cookies, recipe   1789:137
Strawberry shortcake, recipe   1789:136
Swiss fondue, recipe   1789:132

MILK
History of milk   1742:6-7
Milk customs around the world   1742:24-25
Milk use around the world   1742:22-23

MILK—COOKERY
Apple pancakes, recipe   1742:28-29
Cheese toast, recipe   1742:26-27

MILLENNIUM
Countdown calendar, cardboard, crayons, mak-
    ing   2072:6-7
Design a millennium T-shirt, T-shirt, fabric,
    paints, making   2072:26-27
Millennium party, decorations   2072:10-11
Millennograms, walnuts, paper messages, mak-
    ing   2072:8
Time capsule, making   2072:22-23
Time capsule, writing a message and gathering
    possessions, how to do   2014:37
Time idioms, make clock with idiom, pattern
    given   2014:46
Web sites that look into past or future   2072:58-59

Who's Who, 1000-2000 time line, making
2014:34-35

MILLENNIUM—COINS
Preserve a set from 2000, how to do   2072:42-43

MILLENNIUM—COOKERY
Renaissance recipe for salad   2014:25

MILLENNIUM—GAMES
Knucklebones game, how to play   2072:44-45

MILLENNIUM—HANDICRAFTS
25 year calendar, making   2014:13-16
New Year's cards from several countries, making
2014:44-45

MINNESOTA
Activities and books   1918:55-65

MINNESOTA—COOKERY
Spanish spaghetti, recipe   1920:99
Swedish meatballs, recipe   1859:106
Wild rice soup, recipe   1984:91

MINNESOTA—COOKERY—GERMAN. *See also*
WISCONSIN—COOKERY—GERMAN*

MINNESOTA—COOKERY—SWEDISH. *See also*
WISCONSIN—COOKERY—SWEDISH*

MINOANS—MYTHOLOGY
Minotaur head, papier mache, making   1835:34-35

MISSISSIPPI
Activities and books   1918:111-122

MISSISSIPPI—COOKERY
Mississippi mud pie, recipe   1859:71

MISSOURI
Activities and books   1918:55-65

MISSOURI—COOKERY
Black walnut quick bread, recipe   1859:109
Nana's spoon bread, recipe   1920:4

MIXTEC INDIANS
Mixtec codex, paper, watercolor, paints, making
2054:165

MOBILES. *See also* **STABILES***

MOHAWK INDIANS—JEWELRY
Bead necklace, clay, paints, making   2044:107-108

MOLUCCAS. *See* **INDONESIA**

MONET, CLAUDE
Make series of impressionist paintings like
Monet   2184:126-127
Monet paintings of water, autumn colors and
flower gardens, making   2047:16-17

MONGOLIA—FELTMAKING
Handmade felt with quilting, wool, quilting pattern,
making   2218:13-15

MONGOLIA—MUSICAL INSTRUMENTS
Mongolian rattle, making   2108:48-49

MONSTERS. *See also* **DRACULA; FRANKENSTEIN***

MONSTERS—COSTUMES. *See also*
HALLOWEEN—COSTUMES*

**MONTAGUE, JOHN, THE FOURTH EARL OF
SANDWICH**
Activities to celebrate National Sandwich Day;
November 3   1791:46-50

MONTANA
Activities, books   1918:27-39

MONTANA—COOKERY
Cheyenne batter bread, recipe   1859:149

MONTENEGRO. *See* **YUGOSLAVIA**

**MONTENEGRO—HARVEST FESTIVALS—
DOLLS**
Corn doll, dried grass or raffia, lace, making
1846:19

MORAVIA—CHRISTMAS—COOKERY
Christmas bread, recipe   1950:84-85

MORAVIA—HANDICRAFTS
Moravian goose eggs, Slamenky eggs, cardboard,
making   1885:48-49

MOROCCO—COOKERY
Moroccan oranges dish, recipe   2099:22-23
Moroccan pastry balls, recipe   1771:297-298

MOROCCO—FESTIVALS—COOKERY
Feast of the Lamb; couscous, recipe   1903:30-42
Feast of the Lamb; glazed carrots, recipe   1903:39-40
Feast of the Lamb; lamb kebabs, recipe   1903:37-38
Ramadan; date bars, recipe   1903:28-29
Ramadan; mint tea, recipe   1903:30-31
Ramadan; soup, recipe   1903:26-27
Weddings; orange salad, recipe   1903:20-21
Weddings; spiced meatballs, recipe   1903:18-20

MOROCCO—JEWELRY
Enameled pendants, plastic granules, silver wire,
making   1871:10-11

MORRIS, WILLIAM
King Arthur stained glass picture, picture of jewels,
window hanging, making   2048:24-25

MOSES. *See* **BIBLE—HANDICRAFTS—MOSES***

MOTHER GOOSE. *See also* **NURSERY RHYMES***

MOTHER GOOSE DAY
Activities to celebrate   1791:138-143

MOTHER'S DAY
Activities for Mother's Day, patterns   2168:89-100
Activities to celebrate   1791:144-149
Activities to celebrate   1993:79-82
Activities, crafts   1990:79-82
Activities, crafts   1991:75-78
Activities, crafts   1992:75-78
Activities, crafts   1994:79-82
Science, language arts, art, music, math and social
studies activities   2163:317-329

MOTHER'S DAY—COOKERY
French toast, recipe   2185:69
Fruit kabob with yogurt dip, recipe   1790:44-45
Pastel thumbprint cookies, recipe   2058:36

MOTHER'S DAY—DECORATIONS
Balloon vase, paper towel tube, newspaper, making   2128:62-65
Fabric card, old card, fabric, tissue paper, making
2128:60-61
Flowers, flower pots, cards, flower vase decorations, how to make   1882:1-23

63

MOTHER'S DAY—FICTION

Happy Mother's Day by Steven Kroll, activities, patterns, crafts 2183:52-57

The Mother's Day Mice by Eve Bunting, activities, patterns, crafts 2183:46-51

MOTHER'S DAY—HANDICRAFTS

Carnation bouquet, crepe paper, making 2185:71

Hat magnet, fabric, ribbon, decorations, making 2094:111

Perfumed pillow sachet, fabric, potpourri, making 2092:91

Planters for Mother's Day gift, plastic milk jug, plant, soil, making 2093:95

Sachets, fabric, ribbons, dried flowers, making 1790:43

Soap balls, recipe 2185:70

Soap balls, soap flakes, food coloring, making 2094:113

MOTION PICTURES. *See* **MOVIES***

MUHAMMAD, PROPHET. *See also* **MUSLIMS**

MUHAMMAD—BIRTHDAY—COOKERY

Muhammad's birthday cookies, recipe 1771:307-309

MUMMIES. *See also* **EGYPT—ANCIENT**

MUSLIMS—ART—HANDICRAFTS

Dome of the rock picture, gold paint, paper, making 2139:84

MUSLIMS—FESTIVALS—COOKERY

Baby Naming Day; fried plantain, recipe 1819:25

Pumpkin in syrup with pistachios, recipe 2219:21

MUSLIMS—FESTIVALS—SONGS

Eid-ul-Fitr Festival; Eid song 2007:29

MUSLIMS—JEWELRY

Arabesque medallions picture, paper, glue, markers, making 2139:84

MUSLIMS—MINARETS

Minaret towers, miniature model, assorted items, glue, making 2139:86

MUSLIMS—MOSAICS

Ottoman mosaics picture, paper, paints, making 2139:83

MYANMAR. *See* **BURMA***

MYTHOLOGY. *See also* **GREECE, ANCIENT—MYTHOLOGY**

N

67

O

OHIO

Activities and books   1918:67-76

OHIO—COOKERY

Cincinnati chili over pasta, recipe   1859:118-119

Fried apples, recipe   2171:59

Oatmeal cookies, recipe   1920:181

OJIBWA INDIANS. *See also* **CHIPPEWA INDIANS***

OJIBWA INDIANS—COOKERY

Wild rice, recipe   2079:22

OJO-DE-DIOS. *See* **GOD'S EYE**

O'KEEFFE, GEORGIA

Draw and color flower like Georgia O'Keeffe   2184:98-99

O'Keeffe skies, clouds, sunrise and horizons, making   2047:20-21

OKLAHOMA

Activities and books   1918:50-51

OKLAHOMA—COOKERY

Chicken fried steak, recipe   2134:103

Peanut blondie bars, recipe   1859:135

OKTOBERFEST. *See* **GERMANY—FESTIVALS***

OLMEC INDIANS

Olmec stone head model, paper, markers, making   2139:191

Olmec-style stone head, plaster of Paris, making   2114:37

OLYMPICS

Olympic torch, black paper, colored tissue paper, making   1976:16-17

OLYMPICS. *See also* **GREECE, ANCIENT— OLYMPIC GAMES**

OMAN. *See also* **ARABIAN PENINSULA***

OREGON

Activities and books   1918:19-21

OREGON—COOKERY

Cherry pie, recipe   1920:221

Cranberry cookie bars, recipe   1859:172

Frosty fruit smoothie, recipe   2191:65

Hazel nut stuffed pears, recipe   2008:101

OREGON TRAIL—COOKERY

Beans and rice, recipe   1945:27

Boiled potatoes and peas, recipe   1945:11

Cooked greens with bacon and vinegar, recipe   1945:21

Dried apple dumplings, recipe   1945:25

Oregon venison stew, recipe   1945:29

Raspberry-vinegar lemonade, recipe   1945:18

Salt-rising bread, recipe   1945:14-15

Strawberry ice cream, recipe   1945:23

ORIGAMI. *See also* **JAPAN—ORIGAMI**

OTOMI INDIANS—HANDICRAFTS

Amate paper cutouts, pattern, making   2109:71

p

Polar bear, clothespins, craft sticks, white felt, fiber-fill, making   2149:24-25

Seal; mother ringed seal and pup, gray and white socks, plastic bottle, making   2149:30-31

Snowy owl chicks wall hanging, pine cone and fiberfill model, making   2149:16-17

Stoat; summer coat and winter coat stoat, white and brown socks, paper plates, fiberfill, making   2149:34-35

Tern; hand and foot arctic tern, paper model, making   2149:14-15

Walrus mask, paper plate, brown paper, paint, making   2149:22-23

Wolf; snarling wolf face, paper plates, styrofoam cup, making   2149:26-27

POLAR REGIONS—AURORAS

Bottled auroras, plastic soda bottle, sequins, food coloring, making   2149:43

POLLOCK, JACKSON

Make "drip" painting like Jackson Pollock   2184:118-119

POLO, MARCO

Activities from easy to difficult to study life of Marco Polo   2024:3-46

POLYNESIA—COOKERY

Sweet potato pudding, recipe   2099:54-55

POLYNESIA—FLANNEL BOARD STORIES

Felt stories and activities, character patterns, felt board and stand, making   1827:35-45

POMANDERS

Orange, clove and cinnamon pomander ball, making   2030:11

Pomander ball, orange, cloves, spices, ribbon, making   2044:105-106

Potpourri pomander, styrofoam ball, potpourri, making   2161:92-93

POMO INDIANS—COOKERY

Modern Pomo acorn soup, recipe   1826:42

POMO INDIANS—GAMES

Guess the stick guessing game, how to play   2080:22

POOH BEAR. *See* **MILNE, A. A.***

POPCORN

Popcorn Book by Tomie DePaola, activities, patterns   2159:17-28

PORTUGAL—BIRTHDAYS—SONGS

Happy Birthday song to you in Portuguese   1749:46-47

PORTUGAL—COOKERY

Kale soup, recipe   1933:24

PORTUGAL—HANDICRAFTS

Hand painted tiles, tile squares, paints, making   2054:106

PORTUGAL—NEW YEAR'S DAY—HANDICRAFTS

New Year's card, making   2014:44-45

POSADAS. *See* **MEXICO—CHRISTMAS***

POTATOES

History of potatoes   1779:6-9

POTATOES—COOKERY

Potato dishes from around the world   1779:24-25

POTTERY

Coiled worm pot, clay, paints, making   1875:192-193

POULTRY

Customs and beliefs about poultry   1744:24-25

History of poultry   1744:6-9

Poultry cooking around the world   1744:22-23

Poultry dishes from around the world   1744:20-21

POWHATAN INDIANS—GAMES

Shinni game, how to play   1856:22

PRAIRIE. *See* **FRONTIER AND PIONEER LIFE**

PREHISTORIC PAINTINGS

Cave paintings; brown paper, paints, making   1812:31-34

PREHISTORIC PEOPLE—COSTUMES

Cave peoples costumes, making   1798:18-10

PRESIDENTS' DAY

Activities to celebrate   1791:95-99

Activities to celebrate   1993:55-58

Activities, crafts   1990:55-58

Activities, crafts   1991:51-54

Activities, crafts   1992:51-54

Activities, crafts   1994:55-58

PRINCES—PUPPETS

Crown Prince paper pulp and scrap material puppet, making   1764:31-36

PRINCESSES—COSTUMES

Princess costume, making   1798:20-21

PRINCESSES—PARTIES

Invitations, party favors, costumes, games, recipes   1798:20-21

PRINTING. *See also* **POTATOES—PRINTING***

PUBLIC LANDS DAY

Activities to celebrate   1791:205-210

PUEBLO INDIANS—DOLLS

Corn prosperity doll, ears of corn, gourd, feet, making   2212:91-94

Storyteller doll, clay, paints, making   1762:40-45

PUEBLO INDIANS—FOOTWEAR

Moccasins, chamois leather, wax thread, pattern, making   2029:24-25

PUEBLO INDIANS—HANDICRAFTS

Storyteller figure, dough, paint, making   1812:35-38

PUEBLO INDIANS—HOUSES

Adobe bricks from clay, sand and straw, making   2156:22

Hogan model from sticks and clay, making   2212:44-45

Pueblos, shoe box pueblos, making   2139:203

PUEBLO INDIANS—POTTERY

Clay pot, pinched coil method, making   2139:212

Coil bowl, play dough, clay, making   1948:78

Coil pot, clay, ceramic stains, making   2217:41-45

Coil pot, clay, paints, making   2029:22-23

Q

QATAR. *See also* ARABIAN PENINSULA*
QUAKERS—CLOTHING. *See* UNITED STATES
    HISTORY—COLONIAL PERIOD—
    QUAKER*
QUEBEC—COOKERY
    French toast, recipe   1926:26-27
QUEEN CHARLOTTE ISLAND—
    HANDICRAFTS
    Button blanket crest sampler, felt, buttons,
        thread, making   2217:15-17

QUILLING
    Quilled cards, paper, glue, making   2093:93
QUILTING. *See also* PATCHWORK
    Paper quilts, paper scraps, glue, making
        2119:127-130
QUINAULT INDIANS—GAMES
    Stick in the sand game, how to play   1991:14

R

RACERS. *See also* **SKATEBOARDS***

RACKHAM, ARTHUR
Cinderella; Arthur Rackham's illustrations, making 2051:20-21

RAILROADS. *See also* **UNITED STATES— RAILROADS—HISTORY***

RAIN FOREST
Activities and projects to study rain forest theme, patterns 2006:1-48
Great Kapok Tree doorknob hanging tree, paper, pattern, making 1867:31
Great Kapok Tree dramatization; stage, marionettes, animals and human patterns, making 1867:23-26
Great Kapok Tree rain forest environment, how to create trees, plants, canopy, flowers, animals, birds, insects, patterns, making 1867:39-46
Miniature rain forest in terrarium, making 1973:8-9

RAIN FOREST—ANIMALS
Rain forest animals, clay, paints, making 2214:18-19

RAIN FOREST—CANOES
Model dugout canoe, cardboard, clay, paints, making 2214:6-7

RAIN FOREST—COOKERY
Great Kapok Tree; rain forest cookie drops, recipe 1867:41

RAIN FOREST—DIORAMA
Rain forest box, shoe box, soil, felt,, paints, green paper, making 2214:4-5

RAIN FOREST—HOUSES
Maloca community house model, cardboard, burlap, crepe paper, making 2214:10-11

RAIN FOREST—POSTER
Save the Rain forest poster, how to make 2214:22-23

RAIN FOREST—RAIN STICKS
Tropical rain stick, cardboard tube, rice, beans, making 2211:17

RAROTONGA ISLAND—FLANNEL BOARD STORIES
Felt stories and activities, character patterns, felt board and stand, making 1827:35-45

RECYCLING. *See also* **NEWSPAPERS— HANDICRAFTS***; **PAPERMAKING**

RENAISSANCE. *See* **MIDDLE AGES**

RHODE ISLAND
Activities and books 1918:77-85

RHODE ISLAND—COOKERY
Coffee milkshakes, recipe 1859:29
Jonnycakes, recipe 2052:81
Quahog cakes, recipe 2106:100

RICE
Cooking rice, how to do 1745:20-21
Customs and beliefs about rice 1745:22-23
History of rice 1745:6-7
Rice dishes from around the world 1745:24-25

RIVERS—FESTIVALS
Projects, foods, sternwheeler model 1967:33

RIVERS—FESTIVALS—BOATS
Mississippi sternwheeler model, cardboard, making 1967:341-348

RIVERS—FESTIVALS—COOKERY
Stone ground round cookies, recipe 1967:353-354

ROCKS
Rock pile cairns, making 1875:196-197

ROCKY MOUNTAINS—EARLY PEOPLE— HANDICRAFTS
Wrapped twig animals, twigs, thread, raffia, making 2110:12-13

ROMANIA
Gypsy wagon, accordion folded book, making 1868:16-19

ROMANIA. *See also* **GYPSIES**

ROME, ANCIENT—ACTORS—MASKS
Actor's mask, poster paper, paints, patterns, making 1737:29

ROME, ANCIENT—AQUEDUCTS
Cardboard tube and straw aqueduct, making 2180:27

ROME, ANCIENT—BREAD
History of bread 1950:28-32

ROME, ANCIENT—CLOTHING
Toga, man's tunic, fabric, belt, making 1842:13
Toga, man's tunic, old sheet, making 2180:15
Tunica, woman's tunic, cotton sheet, yarn, making 1842:12

ROME, ANCIENT—COOKERY
Bread pudding, recipe 1950:33
Grape punch, recipe 1840:15
Grape punch, recipe 1842:28
Honey omelet, recipe 1842:27
Sweet cheesecake, recipe 2180:11

ROME, ANCIENT—DOLLS
Toy doll, clay, string, making 1842:31

ROME, ANCIENT—FESTIVALS—HANDICRAFTS
Mosaics; Ceres goddess mosaic, patterns, colored papers, glue, making   1737:27
Saturnalia Festival; gift, clay figure, clay, making   1737:29

ROME, ANCIENT—FOOTWEAR
Roman sandals, cardboard, string, making   1978:4-5
Sandals, felt, leather, laces, making   1842:13

ROME, ANCIENT—FRESCOES
Frescoes, plaster of Paris fresco, making   2139:150

ROME, ANCIENT—GAMES
Jackstones game, how to play   1940:38-39
Knucklebone toys, clay, making   1840:6
Knucklebones, clay, making   1842:43

ROME, ANCIENT—HEADWEAR
Laurel wreath, leaves, wire, ribbon, making   1842:14-15

ROME, ANCIENT—JEWELRY
Bracelets, paper, cardboard, gold paint, making   1978:6-7
Brooch, cardboard, paints, making   1842:15
Dolphin brooch, cardboard, gold marker, pattern given, making   1737:26
Snake bracelet, cardboard, paints, making   1840:12-13

ROME, ANCIENT—MOSAICS
Magazine mosaic picture, making   2049:13
Mosaic picture, cardboard, colored paper, making   1978:10-11
Mosaic tile, clay, making   1842:24-25
Mosaic, cardboard, colored paper, making   1840:8
Mosaics, paper mosaics, making   2139:150
Wrapping paper mosaic, making   2049:13

ROME, ANCIENT—MUSICAL INSTRUMENTS
Drum, cardboard, fabric, yarn, making   1840:19
Drum, fabric, cardboard, making   1842:45

ROME, ANCIENT—NUMERALS
Roman numerals, how to write   1978:22-23

ROME, ANCIENT—PULLEYS
Thread spool and string pulley, making   2180:25

ROME, ANCIENT—RELIGION
Healing charm, cardboard, paints, string, making   1840:22-23
Votive offering to leave at Temple, cardboard, paste, wire, making   1842:36

ROME, ANCIENT—ROADS
Groma instrument to check right angles in road building, making   2180:23

ROME, ANCIENT—SOLDIERS
Armored shoes, chicken wire, paper, making   1842:56
Crowns; first over-the-wall crown for soldiers, patterns, making   1737:28
Laurel wreath, cardboard, colored papers, making   1840:26
Legionary soldier's shield, cardboard, paints, making   2180:43

Roman soldier picture, cardboard, crepe paper, foil, making   1978:14-15
Roman soldier shield and sword, cardboard box, red and gold paint, making   1978:18-19
Roman soldier standard emblem, cardboard, red crepe paper, cardboard tubes, making   1978:16-17
Soldier's armor picture, pattern, making   2139:148

ROME, ANCIENT—SPORTS
Marbled pictures of jockey and horses, making   2050:12-13

ROME, ANCIENT—WRITING
Writing tablet and stylus, cardboard, dowel, gold paint, making   1840:16
Writing tablet, balsa wood, string, making   1842:33

ROOSEVELT, THEODORE—FLANNEL BOARD STORIES
Felt stories and activities, character patterns, felt board and stand, making   1827:47-55

ROSE WATER
Rose water, recipe   1820:55

ROSEMALING. *See also* **NORWAY—ROSEMALING**

ROSES
Rose bead necklace, making   1973:11

ROSH HASHANAH—COOKERY
Apples and honey treat, recipe   2185:106
Apples and honey, recipe   2058:7
Challah bread, recipe   1790:71-72
Hallah bread, recipe   2185:104-105
Honey cake, recipe   2133:25
Honey cake, recipe   2185:102-103

ROSH HASHANAH—DECORATIONS
Apple and honey dish, paper plate, cup, making   2154:22-23
Apple New Year card, paper plates, making   2151:24-25
New Year stickers, paper, markers, making   2154:24-25
Wheel of months, cardboard, beads, making   2154:26-27

ROSH HASHANAH—HANDICRAFTS
Shofar pin, yarn, pipe cleaners, making   2154:20
Shofar trivet, cardboard, twine, making   2154:21

ROUSSEAU, HENRI
Rousseau's painting technique with tiger in jungle, how to copy   1770:16-17

RUSSIA
Songs, stories, rhymes, puppets, crafts, patterns   2231:61-83

RUSSIA—ARCHITECTURE
Byzantine domes picture, paper, gold paint, making   2139:114

RUSSIA—ARTISTS
Wassily Kandinsky Imagination Station picture computer project, how to do   2160:84-86

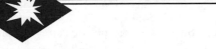

S

SAAMI (PEOPLE)—DRUMS
Magic drum, plywood, leather, making   1914:33-35
SABBATH. *See also* **JEWISH SABBATH; SHABBAT**
SAINT ANDREW'S DAY. *See also* **SCOTLAND—**
FESTIVALS*
SAINT FRANCIS—ART
Stanley Spencer's painting technique when paint-
ing Saint Francis, how to copy   1770:18-21
SAKIA
Sakia model to get water from deep well, spools,
dowels, shoe box, making   2245:22-23
SALISH INDIANS—WEAVING
Salish loom, how to build and use, board, poles
1931:91-93
SALT
Salt paint, recipe   2184:138
SAMHAIN FESTIVAL. *See* **CELTS—FESTIVALS***
SAMOA—HANDICRAFTS
Siapo cloth, brown paper bags, paints, making
2054:147
SAND
3-D puffy sand concoction to make 3-D paint-
ings, recipe   2211:56
Rainbow sand, colored sand mix, making   2211:15
SAND CASTLES
Sand castle clay, recipe   2211:48
SAND PAINTINGS
Sand painting, sand, powdered tempera paints,
cardboard, glue, making   1773:135-137
SANDWICHES
Activities to celebrate National Sandwich Day;
November 3   1791:46-50
SANTA CLAUS. *See also* **CHRISTMAS**
SANTA CLAUS—HANDICRAFTS
Santa pin, metal top, felt, pipe cleaner, pompom,
making   2089:266
SCANDINAVIA. *See also* **DENMARK; FINLAND;**
NORWAY; SWEDEN; VIKINGS
SCANDINAVIA—BREAD
History of bread   1950:36
SCANDINAVIA—COOKERY
Cucumber salad, recipe   2099:74-75
Rye bread, recipe   2027:50-53
SCANDINAVIA—DOLLS
Kitchen witch doll, apple head doll, twigs, dried
grasses, making   1934:40-44
SCANDINAVIA—HANDICRAFTS
Hearts from grass or wheat stalks, making
1934:20-21

SCARECROWS
Build your own scarecrow, boards, old clothes,
making   2157:78
Cornfield scarecrow, paper, pattern, making
2094:36-37
How to design and make a scarecrow   2212:58-60
Pumpkin head scarecrow, pumpkin, stick, old
clothes, making   1854:30-31
Scarecrow from old clothes, sticks, aluminum pie
pans, stuffing, making   1953:48-49
Scarecrow pattern, making   2204:9
Soft sculpture scarecrow, old clothes, straw,
making   1934:123
Traditional scarecrow, old sheet, hat, straw, mak-
ing   1934:120-122
Zuni scarecrow, how to make   2073:131
SCENTS. *See* **PERFUMES***
SCOOTERS. *See* **SKATEBOARDS***
SCOTLAND—BREAD
History of bread in Scotland   1950:68
SCOTLAND—CLOTHING
Plaids, tartan picture, making   2139:172
SCOTLAND—COOKERY
Griddle scones, recipe   2027:86-87
Oatmeal cookies, recipe   1771:101
SCOTLAND—FOLKLORE
Loch Ness monster picture, making   2139:172
SCOTLAND—GARDENS
Portable gardens, large bottle, plants, soil, mak-
ing   2054:103
SCOTLAND—HANDICRAFTS
Kaleidoscope, mylar plastic, tape, making   2054:102
SCOTLAND—HIGHLAND CHIEFTAINS
Badges and mottoes, Highland Chieftains motto
badges, making   2139:173
SCRIMSHAW
Etch a design and highlight it with soot, making
2212:67-68
Scrimshaw pendant, plaster of Paris, making   2055:112
SCULPTURE. *See also* **SAND SCULPTURES***;
SLATE—SCULPTURES*
SEA—PARTIES
Underwater party, invitations, party favors, cos-
tumes, games, recipe   1798:26-27
SEA—PARTIES—COOKERY
Angel fish cake, recipe   1798:57
SEASHELLS. *See* **SHELLS**
SEASHORE. *See also* **SAND**
SEASHORE—HANDICRAFTS
Seaweed pattern   2227:79

SEASONS—FALL. *See* FALL
SEASONS—SPRING. *See* SPRING
SEASONS—SUMMER. *See* SUMMER
SEASONS—WINTER. *See* WINTER
SEMINOLE INDIANS—COOKERY
    Seminole smoothie, recipe   2038:40
SEMINOLE INDIANS—GAMES
    Stickball, how to play   2081:22
SEMINOLE INDIANS—PATCHWORK
    Seminole patchwork design card, colored paper, glue, making   1762:28-33
    Seminole patchwork model, colored paper, patterns, making   1750:93-95
SENEGAL—HATS
    Kufi, fez or crown hat, paper, colored pens, making   1739:21-22
SENUFO (AFRICAN PEOPLE)—HANDICRAFTS
    Mud painting, embroidery hoop, muslin, making 2054:26
SENUFO (AFRICAN PEOPLE)—MUSICAL
    INSTRUMENTS
    Drum, oatmeal box, paper, making   2054:27
SERBIA. *See* YUGOSLAVIA
SHABBAT—HANDICRAFTS
    Challah cover, napkins, yarn, making   2154:14-15
    Foil candleholder, foil, sequins, clay, candles, making   2154:8-9
    Kiddush cup, plastic cups, jewels, stones, glitter, foil, making   2154:12-13
    Napkin covered vase, glass jar, napkins, making 2154:10-11
    Seasonal Tzedakah box, plastic container, felt, decorative trims, making   2154:16-17
    Spice box, plastic tub, foil, spices, making 2154:18-19
SHADOW PUPPETS. *See also* PUPPETS—SHADOW*
SHADUF
    Shaduf model to lift water from well, sticks, stones, clay, making   2245:8-9
SHAKERS—BOXES
    Shaker storage box, cardboard, paints, patterns, making   1967:113-116
SHAKERS—CHRISTMAS—HANDICRAFTS
    Angels, fabric, ribbons, stuffing, making   1846:23
SHAKERS—COOKERY
    Mother Ann's birthday cake, recipe   1967:118-119
    Rose water cookies, recipe   1967:118
SHAKERS—FESTIVALS
    Shaker Festival; food, drama, art, music 1967:102-136
SHAKERS—QUILTS
    Shaker quilt wall hanging, paper model, making 1967:116-117
SHAKERS—VILLAGES
    Model of Shaker village, paper or wooden, making   1967:110-112
SHAVUOT—HANDICRAFTS
    Hoop framed paper cutting, plastic tub and lid, tissue paper, yarn, making   2154:94-95

Moses and the Ten Commandments model, plastic tub, styrofoam ball, paper towels, making 2154:90-91
    Shavuot basket, plastic cap, yarn, pipe cleaner, making   2154:94-95
SHIPS
    Rope for sailing ships in 1700's, making   1934:65-66
SHIPS—FIGUREHEADS
    Model figureheads from baker's dough, making 2212:64-66
SHOSHONE INDIANS—JEWELRY
    Beadwork patterns, how to design, graph, paper, making   1809:40-41
SHROVE TUESDAY. *See also* PANCAKE TUESDAY
SHROVE TUESDAY—COOKERY
    Pancakes, recipe   2230:23
SIAM. *See* THAILAND
SIBERIA—COOKERY
    Siberian dumplings, recipe   1920:109
SICILY—FESTIVALS—COOKERY
    Festival of Santa Rosalia; lemon granita, recipe 1901:36-38
    Festival of Santa Rosalia; mazzarino salad, recipe   1901:35-36
    Festival of Santa Rosalia; milk and nut pudding, recipe   1901:34
    Festival of Santa Rosalia; pasta with tomato sauce, recipe   1901:39-42
SIEGES—COOKERY
    Siege biscuits, recipe   1860:23
SIEGES—TRUCES
    Siege truce, paper soaked in tea, plasticine seal, making   1860:31
SIEGES—WEAPONS
    Mangonel catapult, wood, nails, rubber bands, clay cannon ball, making   1860:9
SIERRA LEONE—EASTER—COOKERY
    Fish pepper soup, recipe   1819:20
SIERRA LEONE—GAMES
    Haba gaba game, how to make and play   1948:183
SIERRA MEWUK INDIANS—GAMES
    Sierra Mewuk dice, walnuts, wax or clay, how to make and play   1934:87-88
SIKHS—COOKERY
    Barfi sweet confection, temple food, recipe 1987:25
SIKHS—FESTIVALS—COOKERY
    Almond burfi dessert, recipe   2007:14
    New Year Baisakhi Festival; chapatis, recipe 1775:28-29
SIKHS—FESTIVALS—HANDICRAFTS
    Raksha Bandham; rakhi bracelets, cardboard, buttons, ribbons, making   2007:14-15
SILVER JEWELRY. *See* NAVAHO INDIANS—
    JEWELRY; PUEBLO INDIANS—JEWELRY*
SIMHATH TORAH—HANDICRAFTS
    Flag for Simhat Torah, dowel, handkerchief, making   2154:52-53
    Torah pin, felt, craft jewels, straw, making 2154:54

SINGAPORE—COOKERY
Singapore steamboat dish, rice, vegetables, beef, fish, shrimp, recipe 1771:351-353

SIOUX INDIANS—CALENDARS
Calendar of events, making 2082:22

SIOUX INDIANS—COUP STICK
Coup stick, jar lid, markers, tree branches, making 2054:128

SIOUX INDIANS—TEEPEES
Tipi, fabric, 8 foot canes, sticks, making 1963:8-9

SIXTIES. *See* **NEW YORK— FESTIVALS— WOODSTOCK***

SKELETONS—PUPPETS
Dancing skeleton puppet, papier mache, springs, paints, making 1764:20-22

SLAVERY
Historical literature, activities, crafts, foods, recipes 2113:71-101

SLAVERY—HISTORICAL FICTION
A Separate Battle by Ina Chang, activities, crafts, foods, recipes 2113:77-79
Charley Skedaddle by Patricia Beatty, activities, crafts, foods, recipes 2113:75-77
Freedom Crossing by Margaret Goff Clark, activities, crafts, foods, recipes 2113:79-81
Runaway to Freedom by Barbara Smucker, activities, crafts, foods, recipes 2113:85-87
Shades of Gray by Carolyn Reeder, activities, crafts, foods, recipes 2113:72-75
The Boys' War by Jim Murphy, activities, crafts, foods, recipes 2113:83-85
The Ghost Wore Gray by Bruce Coville, activities, crafts, foods, recipes 2113:81-83

SLAVES—COOKERY
Hoe cakes, recipe 2020:31
Hoppin' John, black-eyed peas and rice dish, recipe 2003:43
Peanut soup, recipe 2003:42

SLIMES
Flubber slime, non-edible, recipe 2199:192

SLOVAC REPUBLIC. *See* **CZECHOSLOVAKIA**

SLOVAKIA—COOKERY
Ruthenian nut or poppy seed rolls, recipe 1920:6-7

SLOVENIA. *See* **YUGOSLAVIA**

SNOW
Cotton clay for snow sculptures, recipe 2211:45
Snow globe, glass jar, water, glitter, making 2211:74
Snow paint, recipe 2211:65

SNOWFLAKES—PUPPETS
Snowflake finger puppets, patterns, finger plays and creative activities 2070:87-99

SOAP BUBBLES
Bubble mixture, recipe 2088:197

SOUTH AFRICA—BEADS
Message token, bead loom, beads, making 1871:12-13

SOUTH AFRICA—COOKERY
Geelrys, rice dish, recipe 1848:15

Karringmelk beskuit, sweet buttermilk biscuits, recipe 1784:177
Potjiekos, recipe 1811:74-77
Sosaties braai (roast) meat and vegetable dish, recipe 1965:30-31

SOUTH AFRICA—HANDICRAFTS
Bambulina wall hanging, burlap, yarn, making 2054:28

SOUTH AFRICA—JEWELRY
Beaded necklaces, plastic straw, beads, making 1948:111-113

SOUTH AFRICA—KITES
Kite, plastic bag, garden canes, paints, string, making 1965:28-29

SOUTH AFRICA—LANGUAGE
Click languages, how to make click noise 1848:26
Phrases in Afrikaans, isiXhosa, Tshivenda and isiZulu languages 1848:27

SOUTH AFRICA—TOYS
Wire toy, wire, making 2136:31-33

SOUTH AMERICA—COOKERY
Black beans, recipe 2099:114-115
Carmel bananas, recipe 2099:124-125
Corn soup, recipe 2099:110-111
Empanadas, crust filled appetizers, recipe 2099:108-109
Lentil and sausage stew, recipe 2099:116-117
Shredded beef, recipe 2099:120-121

SOUTH AMERICA—HANDICRAFTS
Llama model, papier mache, pattern, making 2109:41

SOUTH AMERICA—JEWELRY
Necklace of creatures, clay, beads, making 1871:14-15

SOUTH AMERICA—PUPPETS
South American bus theater, cardboard, colored paper, making 2179:58-59

SOUTH CAROLINA
Activities and books 1918:111-122

SOUTH CAROLINA—COOKERY
Peach roll, recipe 1859:77

SOUTH DAKOTA
Activities and books 1918:55-65

SOUTH DAKOTA—COOKERY
Cornmeal mush with molasses, recipe 1859:121
Indian tacos, recipe 2102:79

SOUTH KOREA. *See also* **KOREA, SOUTH**

SOUTH KOREA—FESTIVALS—COOKERY
Kkaegangjong sesame seed biscuit, recipe 1988:30-31

SOUTH KOREA—FESTIVALS—HANDICRAFTS
Tan-O-Day; fan, cardboard, flat sticks, making 1988:28-29

SOUTH KOREA—GAMES
Jeki game, how to make and play 1988:26-27
Kongkee, how to make and play 1988:27

SOUTH KOREA—MASKS
Papier mache mask, making 2218:21-23

SRI LANKA—PUPPETS
Hinged puppets, cardboard, straws, making 1948:24-25
ST. DAVID'S DAY. *See* **WALES***
ST. LUCIA'S DAY. *See also* **SWEDEN—CHRISTMAS**
ST. LOUIS—COOKERY
Summer cool cakes, recipe   1920:186
ST. NICHOLAS. *See also* **SANTA CLAUS**
ST. PATRICK'S DAY. *See also* **LEPRECHAUNS***
Activities to celebrate   1791:110-115
Activities to celebrate   1993:63-66
Activities, crafts   1990:59-62
Activities, crafts   1991:55-58
Activities, crafts   1992:55-58
Activities, crafts   1994:63-66
Science, language arts, art, music, math and social studies activities   2163:211-227

ST. PATRICK'S DAY—COOKERY
Eatin' o' the green, cream dip, recipe   2225:158
Emerald cake, recipe   2225:162
Good neighbor potato soup, recipe   1790:23
Leprechaun bars, recipe   2225:159
Lucky clovers, pancakes, recipe   2225:160
Potato cakes, recipe   2185:42
Rainbow pot of gold fruit cups, recipe   2225:161
Shamrock cookies, recipe   2103:30-31
Shamrock rolls, recipe   2053:153
Shamrock shakes, recipe   2058:27
Soda farls, biscuits, recipe   2185:43
Yummy shamrocks, corn flakes, marshmallows, recipe   2086:83

ST. PATRICK'S DAY—DECORATIONS
Bank from sturdy can, making   2093:93
Irish harp mobile, paper, paints, pattern, making 2185:44-45
Leprechaun character, pattern, making   2168:42
Leprechaun with pot of gold, pattern, making 2205:23
Leprechaun, paper, green yarn, pattern, making 2087:56-58
Mr. Shamrock, pattern, making   2168:44
Pot of gold story, pattern, making   2168:43
Rainbow and pot of gold patterns, making 2205:25-26
Shamrock bouquet, paper, pipe cleaners, making 1790:22
Shamrock necklace, modeling clay, paints, sequins, making   2103:28-29
Shamrocks; stand-up shamrocks, pattern, making 2168:41

ST. PATRICK'S DAY—FICTION
Jamie O'Rourke and the Big Potato by Tomie dePaola, activities, patterns, crafts   2183:10-15
St. Patrick's Day in the Morning by Eve Bunting, activities, patterns, crafts   2183:4-9

ST. PATRICK'S DAY—HANDICRAFTS
End of the rainbow stabile, styrofoam ball, jar, fiberfill, making   2152:20-21

Irish castle party favor, tissue tubes, paints, Easter grass, making   2150:42-43
Leprechaun for door, paper, yarn, making 2150:46-47
Leprechaun; hand leprechaun card, paper, paints, making   2150:26-27
Pot of gold table decoration, styrofoam ball, pipe cleaner, fiberfill, making   2150:36-37
Shamrock angel, paper, yarn, gold glitter, making 2150:44-45
Shamrock bird, paper, making   2150:30-31
Shamrock dog pencil holder, tissue tube, felt, making   2150:20-21
Shamrock mouse magnet, felt, yarn, magnet, making   2150:18-19
Shamrock necklace, rigatoni, paper, ribbon, making   2088:268
Shamrock stencils, paper, paint, making   2054:90
Shamrock wand, paper, ribbons, straw, glitter, making   2150:22-23
Shamrock, button-nose shamrock, felt, pipe cleaner, making   2150:16-17
Shamrock, candy boxes, paints, making   2150:10-11
Shamrock, giant shamrock, paper plates, yarn, making   2152:18-19
Shillelagh, tissue paper, egg carton, making 2150:34-35
Snake; chill-chasing snake, fabric, sand, making 1791:112-113
Snake; tube snake, cardboard tube, paint, making 2150:8-9
Stand-up shamrock greeting, cardboard, tissue paper, making   2150:28-29
Stuffed Irish friend, paper stuffed, making 2150:12-13

ST. PATRICK'S DAY—JEWELRY
Bracelet; rainbow bracelet, cardboard tube, pom-poms, ribbon, making   2150:38-39
Necklace; basket of shamrocks necklace, screw caps, yarn, making   2150:24-25
Necklace; lucky penny necklace, bottle caps, yarn, making   2150:40-41

ST. PATRICK'S DAY—MASKS
Leprechaun face mask, paper plates, crepe paper, making   2150:32-33

ST. PATRICK'S DAY—PATTERNS
Leprechaun hat pattern   2226:99-100
Leprechaun pattern   2090:313
Leprechaun pattern   2226:97-98
Pot of gold pattern   2226:101-102
Shamrock pattern   2226:103-104

ST. PATRICK'S DAY—PUPPETS
Irish potato puppet, colored paper, green yarn, making   2150:14-15

ST. VALENTINE'S DAY. *See also* **VALENTINE'S DAY**

STAMPS
Festival of Stamps; Multicultural Festival program, activities, art, crafts, foods, folklore 1771:22-46

STAR OF DAVID
   Wheat or wild grass stalks Star of David, making 1934:22-23
STATUE OF LIBERTY
   Sketches of Statue of Liberty, making   1739:38-39
STONE AGE—ART
   Stone Age pictures using feather or dried grass brushes and natural paints, how to do 1770:8-9
STONE SOUP
   Stone soup, recipe   1797:17
STONES
   Treasure stones, hide small treasure in homemade stone, making   2211:78
SUDAN—BIRTHDAYS—GAMES
   The sheep and the hyena game, how to play 1749:42-43
SUDAN—FACE MAKEUP
   Face paint using hand lotion, paints, how to do 2054:29
   Sudanese face painting, how to do   1812:75-77
SUKKOT—DECORATIONS
   Bird's nest, plastic tub, twine, making   2154:43
   Etrog, foil, bowl, tissue paper, making   2154:46-47
   Fruit and vegetable hammock, net bags, yarn, making   2154:50
   Lulav holder, cardboard tubes, twine, making 2154:49
   My Sukkah collage, paper, fabric, pictures, making   2154:40-41
   Palm willow and myrtle branches, paper tube, tissue paper, making   2154:48
   Sukah hut or booth, cardboard, paints, flowers, twigs, making   1771:367-369
   Sukkah grapes, bubble wrap, felt, making   2154:42
   Sukkah, sticks, clay, leaves, greenery, making 2011:13
   Vine picture holder, green paper, bowl, clothespins, making   2154:44-45
SUKKOT—HANDICRAFTS
   Sukkah, how to build   2236:entire book
SUKUMA (AFRICAN PEOPLE)—FOLKLORE
   How Frog Lost his Tail story with whole language activities   1768:3-9
SULAWESI. *See* **INDONESIA**
SUMATRA. *See* **INDONESIA**
SUMATRA—CALENDARS
   String calendar, heavy paper, string, making 2096:16
SUPERMARKETS. *See* **FOOD; FOOD BUSINESS**
SWAZI (AFRICAN PEOPLE)—BEADS
   Message token, bead loom, beads, making 1871:12-13
SWEDEN—BASKETS
   Paper basket, how to weave   2202:20-21
SWEDEN—CHRISTMAS—DECORATIONS
   Yule box, cardboard, paints, fir branches, making 2202:28-29
SWEDEN—CHRISTMAS—HANDICRAFTS
   Julangel, angel to hang on tree, cardboard, lace, paints, making   2132:28-29

SWEDEN—COOKERY
   Agg Rora, fried egg and milk dish, recipe   1920:28
   Apple crisp, recipe   1920:161
   Coconut chocolate balls, recipe   2132:30-31
   Fruit soup, recipe   2182:81
   Prune pudding, recipe   2201:266
   Sandbakelser (sand tarts), recipe   2054:108-109
   Smorgasbord picture, making   2139:187
   Swedish meatballs, recipe   1920:117
SWEDEN—EASTER—COOKERY
   Lenten buns, recipe   2202:8
SWEDEN—FESTIVALS—COOKERY
   Flag Day or National Day; Jansson's temptation baked sardines and potatoes dish, recipe   2202:19
SWEDEN—FESTIVALS—HANDICRAFTS
   St. Lucia's Day; cardboard candle headdress, making   2139:186
SWEDEN—FLAG
   Pattern of flag   1948:42-43
SWEDEN—FOLKLORE
   Stone Soup flannel board story, felt, patterns given   1767:81-85
SWEDEN—HANDICRAFTS
   Lapland felt square, felt, fabric scraps, making 2054:94
   Oro mobile, straw, yarn, sticks, making   1914:15-17
   Straw ornaments, straw, string, making   2054:107
SWEDEN—LANGUAGE
   Greetings from Sweden   2202:7
SWEDEN—TREES
   Fir trees picture, making   2139:186
SWITZERLAND—BREAD
   History of bread in Switzerland   1950:6
SWITZERLAND—CHRISTMAS—COOKERY
   Anise cookies, recipe   1845:74
   Butter cookies, recipe   1845:74
   Chocolate almond cookies, recipe   1845:75
   Muesli cereal, recipe   1845:75
   Onion tart, recipe   1845:73
   Rosti Swiss potatoes, recipe   1845:73
   Zupfe braided bread, recipe   1845:76
SWITZERLAND—CHRISTMAS—HANDICRAFTS
   Advent tree, chocolates, branch, pot, making 1845:68-69
   Bell ornament, natural materials, moss, seeds, ribbons, making   1845:66-67
   Kissing dove garland, paper, making   1845:65
SWITZERLAND—EASTER—HANDICRAFTS
   Dye; spinach egg dye, making   2054:110
SWITZERLAND—FESTIVALS—MASKS
   Golden leaf mask, foil pan, dry leaves, gold paint, making   2178:18
SWITZERLAND—SCULPTURE
   Giacometti style wire, clay and papier mache sculptures, making   2049:24-25

T

TAHITI—CLOTHING
Grass skirts, raffia, making   2054:148
TAHITI—COOKERY
Firifiri donut, recipe   2120:119
TANZANIA—CLOTH
Printed fabric with symbols, patterns, making
1948:104-108
TANZANIA—COOKERY
Ugali corn porridge, recipe   1966:116
TANZANIA—FLAG
Pattern of flag   1948:42-43
TEDDY BEARS—COOKERY
Apple cake with honey icing, recipe   1967:239-240
Gingerbread bears, recipe   1967:240-241
Honey crunch cookies, recipe   1967:241-242
Honey muffins, recipe   1967:240
TEDDY BEARS—FESTIVALS
Craft projects, foods, picnics, songs, play
1967:223-259
TEDDY BEARS—FLANNEL BOARD STORIES
Felt stories and activities, character patterns, felt
board and stand, making   1827:47-55
TEEPEES
Teepee, full size, making   1931:69-76
TELEGRAPH
Telegraph used in Abraham Lincoln's time, making   1801:30
TELEPHONES
Activities from easy to difficult to study Alexander
Graham Bell's life   2018:2-47
Tin can phone, making   2018:33
TEN COMMANDMENTS. *See* **BIBLE—
HANDICRAFTS—TEN COMMANDMENTS**
TENNESSEE
Activities and books   1918:99-109
TENNESSEE—COOKERY
Fried corn, recipe   1795:76
German potato salad, recipe   1859:80-81
Greens, boiled, recipe   1920:64-65
TENNESSEE—PIONEERS
Log cabin large model, cardboard box, card-
board, making   1967:57-58
TENNESSEE—PIONEERS—COOKERY
Lemon cornmeal cookies, recipe   1967:81-82
Miss Wathe's brownies, recipe   1967:80-81
TENNESSEE—PIONEERS—FESTIVALS
Small Town Heritage Festival; art projects, crafts
and foods   1967:49-101
TEPEES. *See* **TEEPEES**

TERRARIUMS
Rain forest in terrarium, miniature, making
1973:8-9
TEWA INDIANS—COOKERY
Blueberry muffins, recipe   2000:67
TEXAS
Activities and books   1918:45-48
TEXAS—COOKERY
Pedernales river chili, recipe   1814:77
Spicy barbecue sauce, recipe   1859:138
THAILAND—COOKERY
Sweet rice with coconut custard, recipe   1811:85-88
Thai veggie rice noodles, recipe   1926:154-155
THAILAND—FESTIVALS—HANDICRAFTS
Loy Krathong boats, scraps, flowers, leaves,
making   2054:71
THAILAND—GAMES
Elephant log roll, how to play   1948:180
Fish game, how to play   2210:22
THAILAND—JEWELRY
Wish bracelet, yarn, button, beads, making
1948:120-121
THAILAND—SPIRIT HOUSE
House of Spirits, cardboard, paints, making
1807:15
Thai spirit house, making   2108:58-59
Thai spirit house for birds, wood, paints, patterns,
making   1771:339-347
THANKSGIVING. *See also* **PILGRIMS; TURKEYS**
Activities to celebrate   1791:55-59
Activities to celebrate   1993:23-26
Activities, crafts   1990:23-26
Activities, crafts   1991:23-26
Activities, crafts   1992:23-26
Activities, crafts   1994:23-26
Science, language arts, art, music, math and social
studies activities   2163:91-105
THANKSGIVING—COOKERY. *See also*
PILGRIMS—COOKERY
Ambrosia, recipe   1791:59
Apple turkeys, recipe   2058:12
Cornbread squares, recipe   2095:134
Cornbread squares, recipe   2185:121
Cornucopia; mini-pastry cornucopia, recipe
2053:173
Corny pudding, recipe   2225:190
Cranapple cider, recipe   2225:191
Cranberry cloud salad, recipe   2225:192

Cranberry delight, sour cream, gelatin, cranberry
sauce, recipe   2112:29
Pilgrim pies, recipe   2225:193
Popcorn balls, caramel, recipe   2095:135
Pumpkin muffins, recipe   1790:87
Pumpkin pie, recipe   1854:76
Pumpkin pie, recipe   2043:67-68
Three bean salad, recipe   1791:58
Turkey treats, cookies and frosting, recipe   2086:88
Turkey treats, recipe   2225:194
Vegetable cornucopia, recipe   2058:11

THANKSGIVING—DECORATIONS
Cards and envelopes, making   1883:18-21
Hand print turkey, making   1883:8-9
Leaf garland, fall leaves, cord, making   2128:88-89
Turkey card, old card, pattern, making   2128:86-87
Turkey favors, tissue paper, pipe cleaner, making
2088:144
Turkey from cookie dough and candies, pattern,
recipe   2085:16-17
Turkey magnets, button, feathers, felt, making
2092:84
Turkey pins, ice cream spoon, feathers, eyes,
making   2088:144
Turkey; paper bag turkey, making   1883:10-11
Turkey; pine cone turkey, pine cone, paint, paper,
making   2043:64-66
Turkey; pine cone turkey, pine cone, walnut shell,
making   2112:28

THANKSGIVING—DOLLS
Corn husk dolls, pattern, making   2185:123

THANKSGIVING—FICTION
Arthur's Thanksgiving by Marc Brown; litera-
ture, activities, crafts   1898:34-49
Molly's Pilgrim by Barbara Cohen; literature,
activities, crafts   1898:40-45
Sarah Morton's Day by Kate Waters; literature,
activities, crafts   1898:52-57
Sometimes It's Turkey-Sometimes It's Feathers
by Lorna Balian; literature, activities, crafts
1898:58-62
Squanto and the First Thanksgiving by Joyce K.
Kessel; literature, activities, crafts   1898:46-51

THANKSGIVING—GAMES
Bowling for turkeys, decorated plastic bottles,
making   2088:144
Pebble game, how to play   2185:122

THANKSGIVING—HANDICRAFTS
Turkey, stuffed bag with newspaper turkey for
your table, making   2144:last

THANKSGIVING—PATTERNS
Cornucopia pattern   2226:19-20
Native American pattern   2226:21-22
Pilgrim boy and girl pattern   2226:23-26
Pumpkin pie pattern   2226:27-28
Turkey pattern   2226:29-30

THANKSGIVING—PLAYS
Story of the first Thanksgiving theater script
1806:75-82

THANKSGIVING—PUPPETS
Turkey finger puppets, patterns, finger plays and
creative activities   2070:93-95

THAUMATROPES
Bird in a cage thaumatrope, pattern, making
2163:333-339

THEATERS. *See also* **PUPPETS—STAGES***

THREE LITTLE PIGS
Activities and projects to study theme of the
Three Little Pigs, patterns given   1929:1-64

THREE LITTLE PIGS—COOKERY
Applesauce, recipe   1929:64
Hungry pig stew, recipe   1929:64
Snout cookies, recipe   1929:64

TIBET—COOKERY
Yogurt and rice dessert, recipe   2216:21

TIBET—JEWELRY
Beads, clay, wool, yarn, paints, making   2216:12-13
Necklace and earrings, making   2108:44-45

TIBET—LANGUAGE
Greetings from Tibet   2216:7

TIBET—MASKS
Tibetan mask, cardboard, paints, making
2216:28-29

TIBET—MUSICAL INSTRUMENTS
Tibetan lama gong, making   2108:52-53

TIBET—RELIGION
Prayer flag, white cloth, colored markers, making
1812:45-48

TIE DYE
Pencil cases, tie-dye, fabric, fabric dye, making
2092:95
Tie-dyeing cloth, how to do   2212:160-163

TIME CAPSULES
Personal time capsule with stab-binding, making
1868:20-22
Time capsule, how to prepare and bury
1952:134-135

TIN CANS. *See* **RECYCLING**

TIPI. *See* **TEEPEES**

TLINGIT INDIANS—FOOTWEAR
Tlingit style moccasins, leather, yarn, felt, making   1934:82-86

TLINGIT INDIANS—TOTEM POLES
Stacking totem pole, cardboard containers,
paints, making   1948:63-65

TLINGIT INDIANS—WEAPONS
Armor, corrugated paper, making   2139:207

TOBAGO—MUSICAL INSTRUMENTS
Steel drum, tin cans, rubber bands, making
1948:154

TOGO—RAIN STICKS
Rain stick, paper towel tube, paper, nails, rice,
making   2140:20-21

U

UFO'S
Flying saucer with launch pad, plastic bottles, paper plates, straws, foil, making   1935:16-17
UFO Days – July; activities to celebrate flying saucers   2175:54-61

UKRAINE—COOKERY
Chicken kyiv, recipe   1752:121
Kugel, recipe   2099:86-87
Pierogies, egg, flour, potatoes, recipe   1920:82

UKRAINE—EASTER—HANDICRAFTS
Egg dyeing, how to do   2186:20-21
Pysanky eggs, dyes, wax, making   1934:94-98

UNDERGROUND RAILROAD
Activities from easy to difficult to study life of Harriet Tubman   2020:2-47

UNDERGROUND RAILROAD—QUILTING
Log cabin quilt based on underground railroad, paper, pattern, making   1911:12-13

UNITED ARAB EMIRATES. *See also* **ARABIAN PENINSULA***

UNITED KINGDOM OF GREAT BRITAIN. *See* **ENGLAND; IRELAND; SCOTLAND; WALES**

UNITED NATIONS DAY
Activities to celebrate United Nations Day   1791:34-39
Activities, crafts   1992:15-18

UNITED STATES
Folk tales, celebrations, arts and crafts, foods, activity pages, games   2201:381-437

UNITED STATES—1600'S—BREAD
History of bread   1950:39-40

UNITED STATES—1700'S—BREAD
History of bread   1950:50

UNITED STATES—1800'S—BREAD
History of bread   1950:58-59

UNITED STATES—1900'S—BREAD
History of bread   1950:71-73

UNITED STATES—1930'S—BREAD
History of bread   1950:70

UNITED STATES—ARTISTS
Burchfield pictures in wintry colors, making   2047:24-25
Georgia O'Keeffe A Bee's Eye View flower picture computer project, how to do   2160:87-89
O'Keeffe skies, clouds, sunrise and horizons, making   2047:20-21
Walt Disney bad hair day cartoon computer project, how to do   2160:94-95

Walt Disney dancing pixels cartoon computer project, how to do   2160:92-93
Walt Disney twirling lollipop cartoon computer project, how to do   2160:91

UNITED STATES—COOKERY
Apple pie, recipe   2099:106-107
Applesauce, recipe   2201:417
Baked apple, recipe   2201:416
Banana bread, recipe   1775:26-27
Bread from wheat berries, recipe   2125:15-17
Bubble bread, recipe   2027:128-130
Cajun cornmeal fritters (coush-coush), recipe   2201:417
Carrot cake, recipe   1778:28-29
Chicken, lemon chicken, recipe   1744:26-27
Cinnamon rolls, recipe   1920:13
Country-style chicken and gravy, recipe   2099:96-97
Cranberry nut bread, recipe   2002:65
Croutons, recipe   1950:78
Dilly casserole bread, recipe   1920:9
Eggs in a nest, recipe   2201:420
Fruitsicles, recipe   2201:419
Grandma's biscuits, recipe   1920:11
Granola, recipe   1916:147
Haddock, creamy baked, recipe   1777:26-27
Hamburger on a bun, recipe   2201:414
Hush puppies, recipe   2201:419
Ice cream soda, recipe   1811:19-20
Ice cream soda, recipe   2201:415
King cake, recipe   1784:189
Macaroni and cheese, recipe   1811:79-81
Oatmeal school cookies, recipe   2000:88
Omelette souffle, lemon, recipe   1776:28-29
Potato boats, recipe   2201:413
Potato pie, recipe   1779:28-29
Potato, baked and stuffed with eggs and cheese, recipe   1779:26-27
Ratatouille vegetable dish, recipe   1778:26-27
Shortcake, recipe   1916:143
Shrimp-filled baked potatoes, recipe   1777:28-29
Snickerdoodles, recipe   2201:419
Turkey sandwich, recipe   2201:418
Waldorf salad, recipe   2201:416
White bread, recipe   1950:73
Yeast bread, recipe   1784:189

UNITED STATES—DOLLS
Raggedy Ann and Andy, paper plate and yarn dolls, making   2087:136

91

New England clam chowder, recipe   2003:23
New World cocoa mix, recipe   1824:55
Ole kooks, recipe   1789:23
Philadelphia pepper pot, recipe   1874:29
Porridge, recipe   1789:21
Potato cakes with rosemary, recipe   2003:24
Pound cake, recipe   1824:42
Pumpkin pie, recipe   1824:51-52
Pumpkin soup, recipe   2003:28
Queen cakes, recipe   1783:8
Spanish rice, recipe   1824:53-54
Spiced cider, recipe   1824:43
Spring vegetable and herb soup, recipe   2003:29
Squash soup, recipe   1789:25
Steamed clams, recipe   1824:49-50
Stewed pumpkin, recipe   1789:26
Succotash, recipe   1789:26
Twelfth Night cake, recipe   1783:15
Wax sugar, maple syrup, recipe   2003:52

UNITED STATES—HISTORY—COLONIAL PERIOD—DANCES

Minuet, how to do   1783:14

UNITED STATES—HISTORY—COLONIAL PERIOD—DOLLS

Apple face doll, apple, pipe cleaners, making 2054:130
Corn husk dolly, corn husks, yarn, making 1824:125-126
Corncob doll, corncob, fabric, making   2044:75-76
Puppet doll, sock, stuffing, flannel, making 1824:128-129
Spoon doll, spoon, fabric, making   1824:127

UNITED STATES—HISTORY—COLONIAL PERIOD—DYES

Cranberry, walnut and mustard dyes, making 1916:156
Dye a shirt or socks, onion skin dye, making 1824:101
Dyeing a rainbow book, how to do   1851:22-23

UNITED STATES—HISTORY—COLONIAL PERIOD—FOLKLORE

Home: A Journey Through America by Thomas Locker, activities and recipes for the classroom   1916:142-144
The Seasons Sewn by Whitford, activities and recipes for the classroom   1916:154-157

UNITED STATES—HISTORY—COLONIAL PERIOD—GAMES

Bilbo catcher, how to play   1824:118
Bilboquest game of cup and ball, how to make and play   1783:12
Blindman's bluff, how to play   2044:77-78
Bubble blowers, how to make and play   2044:78-79
Frog in the middle, how to play   1783:10
Game of graces, how to play   1783:10
Hide the thimble, how to play   1783:11
Hide the thimble, how to play   1824:116

Honey pot, how to play   1824:115
Hoop race, how to play   1783:10
Hoop roll, how to play   1824:114
Hopscotch, how to play   1824:117
Horseshoe pitching, how to play   1824:121
Hunt the ring, how to play   1783:11
Jacks, how to play   2044:39-41
Jackstraws, also called spillikin, sticks or straws, how to make and play   2044:94
Leapfrog, how to play   1824:119
Nine Men Morris, how to play   2014:29
Ninepins, how to play   1824:124
Queen Anne and her maids, how to play   1783:11
Quoits, similar to horseshoes, how to play 2044:42-43
Shooting marbles, how to play   1824:120
Tag – you're it, how to play   1824:122
Twirl a top, how to play   1824:123

UNITED STATES—HISTORY—COLONIAL PERIOD—HANDICRAFTS

Appliqued picture, fabric, felt, glue, pattern, making   2044:103-104
Corker of a pot holder, yarn, making   2161:174-175
Corker; making a corker, tube, nails, felt scraps, how to do   2161:170-171
Corking, yarn, how to do   2161:172-173
Decoupage box, making   1824:96
Embroidered colonial wall pocket, paper, crayon, making   1851:12-13
Embroidered computer sampler, making   1851:30-31
Embroidered cross stitch place card, paper, crayon, making   1851:26-27
Embroidered sampler card with verse, sampler card, pattern given, making   1851:34-35
Embroidery, how to do   2161:200
Friendship battledore, pattern given, paper, making   1851:12-13
Lantern; tin lantern, tin can, paints, candle, making   1773:130-131
Marbled paper, paper, paints, making   2044:50-51
Papyrotamia, paper cutting gifts, how to make 1783:13
Pompom bunny, yarn, making   2161:168
Pompom yard animals, yarn, making   2161:169
Pompoms, yarn, how to do   2161:166-167
Quill pen, feather, making   2044:52-53
Rag rug, fabric strips, thread, making   1824:28-29
Rugs; rag rugs, picture frame, old fabric, progger tool, making   2200:30-31
Sachet, fabric, ribbon, potpourri, making   2044:36-37
Stenciled note cards, paper, envelopes, stencils, paints, making   2044:100-102
Stenciling, cardboard, fabric, paint, making 2161:182-185
Sundial, cardboard, paint, compass, making 2044:9-11
Wool; dyeing wool, how to do   2043:24-27

V

Tet Trung-Thu Festival; lantern, paper, cardboard tube, making 2054:72

VIETNAM—FOLKLORE
The Strongest in the Forest story with whole language activities 1768:20-25

VIETNAM—GAMES
Elephant march game, how to play 1948:182

VIETNAM—KITES
Vietnamese kite, paper, sticks, making 1948:47-49

VIETNAM—LANTERNS
Paper lantern, paper, tape, pattern given, making 1948:30-31
Plastic lid lantern, pattern given, making 1948:32-33

VIETNAM—NEW YEAR—COOKERY
Asparagus soup, recipe 2239:17-18
Glass noodle salad, recipe 2239:19-22
Spring rolls, recipe 2223:13
Vietnamese bananas, recipe 2239:22-23

VIETNAM—NEW YEAR—HANDICRAFTS
Tet Nguyen-den greeting cards, cotton fabric, cardboard, watercolor, paints, making 2223:10-11
Tet Nguyen-den paper blossoms, tissue paper, branch, making 2223:15

VIKINGS—CLOTHING
Woman's cap, cloth, ribbon, making 1980:33

VIKINGS—COMBS
Antler comb, cardboard, clay, making 1843:22-23
Comb from an antler, making 1980:26

VIKINGS—COOKERY
Butter oats biscuits, recipe 1980:11

VIKINGS—FOOTWEAR
Viking shoes, felt, thread, making 1980:27

VIKINGS—GAMES
Nine Men Morris, how to play 2014:29
Viking ball, fabric, making 1843:27

VIKINGS—HOUSES
Viking long houses, shoe box long house, making 2139:180
Viking longhouse, shoe box, paints, cardboard, making 2215:10-11

VIKINGS—JEWELRY
Amber necklace, paper, toothpicks, paints, making 1980:39
Brooches, foil, gold beads, making 2215:4-5

VIKINGS—LANGUAGE
Runic alphabet, Viking Runes picture, making 2139:183
Viking letters; runes, plaque, cardboard, paints, making 2215:22-23
Viking runes chart 1843:25

VIKINGS—METAL WORK
Metalcraft, ornaments model, clay, paints, making 2139:184

VIKINGS—MYTHOLOGY
Thor's hammer, clay, silver and bronze paints, making 1843:16
Thor's hammer, clay, wooden board, cord or ribbon, making 2215:20-21

VIKINGS—SHIPS
Dragon figurehead for ship, papier mache, cardboard tube, paints, making 2215:14-15
Longboat, powered, plastic bottle, paper tubes, making 1935:8-9
Longships picture, paper, foil, pattern, making 2139:180
Viking ship, cardboard, dowels, paints, making 1980:19

VIKINGS—WARRIORS
Helmet, papier mache over balloon, paints, making 2140:14-15
Helmet, papier mache, paints, making 1980:43
Helmets; ceremonial helmets, paper Viking helmet, making 2139:182
Helmets; Viking battle helmets, cardboard, aluminum foil, making 2139:182
Raven banner, red cardboard, black paper, making 1843:21
Shield, cardboard, plastic container, paints, making 1980:42
Viking shield, poster board shield, making 2139:182
Viking warrior ax and shield, cardboard tube, paints, pie pan, making 2215:16-17
Viking warrior picture, foil, colored paper, felt scraps, making 2215:6-7

VIKINGS—WEAPONS
Battle ax, cardboard ax, making 2139:183
Battle ax, dowel, cardboard, making 1843:15

VIKINGS—WOODCARVING
Woodcarvings, wood or styrofoam carving, making 2139:183

VIKINGS—WOOL
Tool brooch to comb burrs out of wool, how to make 1843:12-13

VIRGINIA
Activities and books 1918:99-109

VIRGINIA—COOKERY
Chocolate chess pie, recipe 1796:70
Virginia ham with cherry sauce, recipe 1859:83

VOLCANOES—COOKERY
Volcano cake, recipe 1798:54

W

WALES—COOKERY
Honey cake (Teisen Fel), recipe   1771:100
Welsh pasties, recipe   1920:114-115

WALES—HANDICRAFTS
Spoon; Welsh love spoon, cardboard, papier mache, paints, patterns, making   1771:87-93

WALES—SYMBOLS
Red dragons symbol picture, pattern, making 2139:170-171

WAMPANOAG INDIANS—COOKERY
Dried corn, recipe   1916:53

WAMPANOAG INDIANS—FOLKLORE
Tapenum's Day: A Wampanoag Indian Boy in Pilgrim Times by Kate Waters, activities and recipes for the classroom   1916:51-53

WAMPANOAG INDIANS—GAMES
Ring and pin target practice game, how to play 2082:22

WAMPUM. *See also* **IROQUOIS INDIANS; WOODLAND INDIANS**

WANJI WANJI, SUSAN
Australian aboriginal artist, how to copy her techniques   1770:26-29

WARPLANES. *See* **AIRPLANES***

WASHINGTON (STATE)
Activities, books   1918:16-18

WASHINGTON (STATE)—COOKERY
Baked apples, recipe   1859:175
Chinese noodles, recipe   1920:102
Yakima apple pie, recipe   2192:66

WASHINGTON, DC—COOKERY
Senate bean soup, recipe   1887:77

WASHINGTON, GEORGE
Activities to study the life of George Washington 1850:3-46

WASHINGTON, GEORGE—COOKERY
Cherry tarts, easy recipe   2185:39
Cherry tree pillow, puff pastry, recipe   2053:151
George's corn cakes, recipe   1790:11
Indian hoecakes, recipe   2233:45

WASHINGTON, GEORGE—DECORATIONS
Corn and salt modeling dough, making   1790:10

WASHINGTON, GEORGE—FICTION
George Washington's Breakfast by Jean Fritz, activities, crafts   2233:44-49

WASHINGTON, GEORGE—HATS
George Washington hat, paper, ribbon, making 2153:52-53
Three-cornered hat pattern   2226:93-94

Tri-cornered hat, pattern, making   2233:49

WASHINGTON, GEORGE—PATTERNS
Cherry pattern   2226:91-92
Washington silhouette pattern   2226:95-96

WASHINGTON, GEORGE—PUPPETS
Stick puppets, paper, pattern, making   2207:34

WEATHER VANES
Wood or cardboard weather vane, making 2212:53-54

WEAVING
Plant weaving, use reed and rush leaves to make mats, how to do   1875:188-189
Standing loom, how to make   2212:166-168

WEBSTER, NOAH
Activities to celebrate Dictionary Day; October 16   1791:24-27

WEST (U.S.)
Activities and books   1918:13-25

WEST (U.S.)—COOKERY
Buffalo or beef jerky, recipe   1943:15
California date walnut bread, recipe   1789:161
California smoothie drink, recipe   1789:168
Cherry sauce, recipe   1943:17
Cioppino, fish stew, recipe   1789:167
Cobb salad, recipe   1789:165
Corn and beans with sunflower nuts, recipe   1943:23
Crab Louis, recipe   1789:166
Denver omelet, recipe   1789:161
Filbert crescents, recipe   1789:168
Fresh Colorado trout, recipe   1789:166
Fruit soup, recipe   1789:164
Hawaiian chicken, recipe   1789:163
Hawaiian yams, recipe   1789:163
Hominy and bacon, recipe   1943:11
Meat soup, recipe   1943:25
Pan-fried catfish, recipe   1943:13
Pecan waffles, recipe   1789:162
Roasted Jerusalem artichokes, recipe   1943:19
Salmon loaf, recipe   1789:165
Smoked salmon soup, recipe   1943:25
Steak and eggs, recipe   1789:161

WEST INDIES—FOLKLORE
Spiders Tug of War flannel board story, felt, patterns given   1767:116-121

WEST VIRGINIA
Activities and books   1918:99-109

WEST VIRGINIA—COOKERY
Apple butter, recipe   1899:106
Fried ramps (leeks), recipe   1989:80

Golden delicious apple pie, recipe   1859:86-87

WESTWARD MOVEMENT

Historical literature, activities, crafts, foods, recipes   2113:102-129

WESTWARD MOVEMENT—COOKERY

Baked beans, recipe   1789:56

Baking soda biscuits, recipe   1789:55

Corn fritters, recipe   1789:55

Cowboy frying pan bread, recipe   1789:56

Cowboy pie, recipe   1789:57

Cranberry jelly, recipe   1789:58

Prospector's grub, bacon, beans, sardines, recipe   1896:15

Red beans and rice, recipe   1896:21

Skillet bread, recipe   1896:9

Sourdough biscuits, recipe   1789:55

Sourdough pancakes, recipe   1789:54

Sourdough starter, recipe   1789:53

Sun-dried fruit, recipe   1789:53

Tacos, recipe   1789:57

Wilted lettuce salad, recipe   1789:58

WESTWARD MOVEMENT—LUMBER CAMPS—COOKERY

Corned beef and boiled potatoes, recipe   1905:11

Hot roast beef sandwiches, recipe   1905:19

Mashed potatoes and gravy, recipe   1905:23

Molasses cookies, recipe   1905:29

Oatmeal bread, recipe   1905:17

Raisin pie, recipe   1905:25

Sourdough pancakes, recipe   1905:15

Sourdough starter, recipe   1905:14

Split pea soup, recipe   1905:27

WHEAT

Wheat berries ground to make flour for bread, recipe   2125:15-17

Wheat swag, wheat stalks, thread, ribbon, making   2030:37

WHITTLING

Soap carved sculpture, making   1875:198

Whimmy diddle toy, make from branch   1875:199

Whistle from green tree bark, making   1875:200-201

WIGWAMS. *See also* **WOODLAND INDIANS**

WILD WEST. *See* **COWBOYS; WESTWARD MOVEMENT**

WILDER, LAURA INGALLS—BROOMS

Ma's willow-bough broom, stick, willow branches, twine, making   1852:16-17

WILDER, LAURA INGALLS—CLOTHING

Laura's woolen hood and muffler, wool fabric, thread, making   1852:46-49

Mary's Christmas tassel for slippers, cardboard, yarn, making   1852:38-39

WILDER, LAURA INGALLS—COOKERY. *See also* **FRONTIER AND PIONEER LIFE— COOKERY**

Laura's wheat-sheaf light bread, recipe   1852:60-63

WILDER, LAURA INGALLS—DOLLS

Laura's corncob doll, corncob, corn husks, fabric, making   1852:8-11

Laura's doll's apron, fabric, ribbon, pattern, making   2010:42-47

WILDER, LAURA INGALLS—FLOWERS

Little Town orange flowers, oranges, making   1852:54-55

WILDER, LAURA INGALLS—FUEL

Pa and Laura's hay sticks, hay or raffia, making   1852:44-45

WILDER, LAURA INGALLS—GARDENS

Ma's prairie garden, how to plant vegetable garden   1852:18-21

WILDER, LAURA INGALLS—HANDICRAFTS

Alice's embroidered sampler, fabric, thread, frame, making   2010:36-42

Alice's straw air-castle, wheat straws, wire, fabric, making   1852:26-29

Carrie's lace-edged handkerchief, fabric, lace, making   2010:22-25

Laura's embroidered picture frame, wool floss, perforated paper, making   2010:30-35

Little Town party napkins, cloth napkins, how to fold   1852:52-53

Ma's cross-stitched bread cloth, fabric, embroidery thread, making   1852:40-43

Ma's embroidered pillow sham, fabric, embroidery thread, making   1852:22-25

Ma's needle book, fabric, ribbon, embroidery thread, pattern, making   2010:12-15

WILDER, LAURA INGALLS—HATS

Charlotte's straw hat, straw or raffia, thread, ribbon, making   1852:12-15

Laura's prairie sunbonnet, fabric, ribbon, elastic, pattern, making   2010:48-59

WILDER, LAURA INGALLS—JEWELRY

Mary's beaded bracelet and ring, beads, thread, making   1852:58-59

WILDER, LAURA INGALLS—LAMPS

Ma's button lamp, button, thread, making   1852:50-51

Mary's beaded lamp mat, woven braid or cord, beads, making   1852:56-57

WILDER, LAURA INGALLS—QUILTING

Laura's bear's track quilted pillow, fabric, stuffing, making   1852:32-33

Laura's nine-patch pillow, fabric, thread, stuffing, pattern, making   2010:16-21

WILDER, LAURA INGALLS—RUGS

Mary's braided rug, fabric, clothespins, making   2010:26-29

WILDER, LAURA INGALLS—TOYS

Carrie's baby button string, buttons, heavy thread, making   1852:30-31

XHOSA (AFRICAN PEOPLE)—JEWELRY
Drinking straw and beaded necklaces, making
1948:111-113

YAKURR (AFRICAN PEOPLE)—HARVEST FESTIVALS—COOKERY
Leboku Harvest Festival; yam fufu, recipe   2122:9

YANOMAMO INDIANS—ANIMALS
Rain forest animals, clay, paints, making
2214:18-19

YANOMAMO INDIANS—BEADS
Colorful beads, clay, thread, paints, making
2214:12-13

YANOMAMO INDIANS—CANOES
Model dugout canoe, cardboard, clay, paints,
making   2214:6-7

YANOMAMO INDIANS—DIORAMA
Rain forest box, shoe box, soil, felt, paints, green
paper, making   2214:4-5

YANOMAMO INDIANS—HEADDRESSES
Headdress, cardboard, crepe paper, paints, making   2214:16-17

YANOMAMO INDIANS—HOUSES
Maloca community house model, cardboard,
burlap, crepe paper, making   2214:10-11

YANOMAMO INDIANS—POSTER
Save the rain forest poster, how to make   2214:22-23

YAQUI INDIANS—EASTER
Rattles for Easter dances, orange, papier mache,
making   1846:15

YAQUI INDIANS—JEWELRY
Headdress, straws, thread, homemade beads,
making   1948:115-117

YAQUI INDIANS—MUSICAL INSTRUMENTS
Drum, tin can, making   1948:150-151

YEMEN. *See also* ARABIAN PENINSULA*

YOM KIPPUR—DOLLS
Outside me and inside me doll, paper, making
2154:30-31

YOM KIPPUR—GAMES
Jonah into the whale flip game, sock, cup, yarn,
clothespins, making   2151:26-27

YOM KIPPUR—HANDICRAFTS
Book of life, old book, gold paint, ribbon, making   2154:36
Jonah and the whale water toy, plastic bottle,
making   2154:32-33
Shofar, brown paper bag, party horn, making
2154:38
Yahrzeit candleholder, making   2154:37

YOM KIPPUR—PUPPETS
Jonah and the whale puppet, paper, yarn, making
2154:34-35

YORUBA (AFRICAN PEOPLE)—ADIRE CLOTH
Painted pictures on fabric, wax, crayon, picture
frame, fabric dye, making   2200:18-19

YORUBA (AFRICAN PEOPLE)—HANDICRAFTS
Metal casting, foil, plaster of Paris, making
2054:33
Tie-dye top, fabric, dyes, string, making   2054:34-35

YUGOSLAVIA—COOKERY
Potica dessert with walnut tarragon or chocolate
filling, recipe   2199:164-166

Z

ZAMBIA—BASKETS
Coil baskets, yarn, glue, paint, making   2139:68
Colorful baskets, fabric, making   2054:15
ZAMBIA—COOKERY
Nshima with peanut chicken (polenta type cornmeal mush with chicken dish), recipe   1754:121
ZAMBIA—PROVERBS
Zambian proverbs   1754:81
ZIMBABWE—COOKERY
Dovi chicken stew, recipe   2201:26
Fried plantains, recipe   2201:26
ZODIAC
Projects, crafts, foods   1967:137-166
ZODIAC—COOKERY
Zodiac cookies, recipe   1967:161-162
ZULUS—BASKETS
Children's oops basket, plastic cup, yarn, making   1812:61-64
ZULUS—BEADS
Message token, bead loom, beads, making   1871:12-13

ZULUS—GAMES
Stone throw game, how to play   1948:165
ZULUS—WEAPONS
Zulu spear and shield, cardboard shield, paints, making   2139:70
ZUNI INDIANS—COOKERY
Blueberry muffins, recipe   2000:67
ZUNI INDIANS—GAMES
Wood cans (ta:sholi:we) game, how to make and play   2062:42-43
ZUNI INDIANS—GARDENING
More sisters, sunflowers, beans and pumpkins, how to grow   2073:126-132
Three Sisters of Life garden of corn, beans, and squash, how to do   2073:120-125
ZUNI INDIANS—SCARECROWS
Zuni scarecrow, how to make   2073:131

Books Indexed by Number

See "Books Indexed by Author" for an alphabetical list of books by author.

1771. Heath, Alan. *Windows on the World: Multi-cultural Festivals for Schools and Libraries*. Metuchen, New Jersey, The Scarecrow Press, 1995.

1772. Ganeri, Anita. *Buddhist*. Danbury, Connecticut, Childrens Press, 1997.

1773. Anderson, Alan H. *Geology Crafts for Kids*. New York, Sterling Publishing Co., 1996.

1774. Bonvielain, Nancy. *The Navajos: People of the Southwest*. Brookfield, Connecticut, The Millbrook Press, 1995.

1775. Powell, Jillian. *Bread*. Austin, Texas, Steck-Vaughn Publishers, 1996.

1776. Powell, Jillian. *Eggs*. Austin, Texas, Steck-Vaughn Publishers, 1997.

1777. Powell, Jillian. *Fish*. Austin, Texas, Steck-Vaughn Publishers, 1997.

1778. Powell, Jillian. *Vegetables*. Austin, Texas, Steck-Vaughn Publishers, 1997.

1779. Powell, Jillian. *Potatoes*. Austin, Texas, Steck-Vaughn Publishers, 1997.

1780. Dawson, Imogen. *Clothes and Crafts in Aztec Times*. Parsippany, New Jersey, Dillon Press, 1997.

1781. Altman, Linda Jacobs. *California*. Tarrytown, New York, Marshall Cavendish, 1997.

1782. *Amazing Activities and Things to Do*. New York, Anness Publishing Co., 2000.

1783. *American Girls Party Book*. Middleton, Wisconsin, Pleasant Company Publications, 1998.

1784. Angell, Carole S. *Celebrations Around the World: A Multicultural Handbook*. Golden, Colorado, Fulcrum Publishing, 1996.

1785. *Arts and Crafts for Little Hands, Preschool-Grade 1*. Greensboro, North Carolina, Education Center, 1997.

1786. Ayer, Eleanor H. *Colorado*. Tarrytown, New York, Marshall Cavendish, 1997.

1787. Balkwill, Richard. *Clothes and Crafts in Ancient Egypt*. Parsippany, New Jersey, Dillon Press, 1998.

1788. Baldwin, Guy. *Wyoming*. Tarrytown, New York, Marshall Cavendish, 1999.

1789. Barchers, Suzanne I. *Cooking up U.S. History: Recipes and Research to Share with Children*. 2nd ed. Englewood, Colorado, Teacher Ideas Press, 1999.

1790. Barchers, Suzanne I. *Holiday Storybook Stew—Cooking Through the Year with Books Kids Love*. Golden, Colorado, Fulcrum Publishing, 1998.

1791. Barkin, Carol. *The Holiday Handbook: Activities for Celebrating Every Season of the Year and More*. New York, Clarion Books, 1993.

1792. Barlas, Robert. *Jamaica*. Milwaukee, Wisconsin, Gareth Stevens Publishing, 1998.

1793. Barr, Marilynn G. *Storybook Patterns*. Palo Alto, California, Monday Morning Books, 1995.

1794. Barrett, Tracy. *Kentucky*. Tarrytown, New York, Marshall Cavendish, 1999.

1795. Barrett, Tracy. *Tennessee*. Tarrytown, New York, Marshall Cavendish, 1998.

1796. Barrett, Tracy. *Virginia*. Tarrytown, New York, Marshall Cavendish, 1997.

1797. Bass, Jules. *Cooking with Herb, the Vegetarian Dragon*. New York, Barefoot Books, 1999.

1798. Bastyra, Judy. *Parties for Kids*. New York, Kingfisher, 1998.

1799. Berg, Elizabeth. *Nigeria*. Milwaukee, Wisconsin, Gareth Stevens Publishing, 1998.

1800. Berry, Carrie. *A Confederate Girl: The Diary of Carrie Berry, 1864*. Mankato, Minnesota, Blue Earth Books, 2000.

1801. Binder, Amy. *Abraham Lincoln*. Irving, Texas, Living History Productions, 1993.

1802. Binder, Amy. *Florence Nightingale*. Irving, Texas, Nest Entertainment, 1993.

1803. Binder, Amy. *Thomas Edison and the Electric Light*. Irving, Texas, Living History Productions, 1993.

1804. Bircher, William. *A Civil War Drummer Boy: The Diary of William Bircher, 1861-1865*. Mankato, Minnesota, Blue Earth Books, 2000.

1805. Blashfield, Jean F. *Wisconsin*. Danbury, Connecticut, Childrens Press, 1998.

1806. Blau, Lisa. *Fall Is Fabulous*. Bellevue, Washington, One From the Heart Educational Resources, 1994.

1807. Bliss, Helen. *Models*. New York, Crabtree Publishing Company, 1998.

1808. Bliss, Helen. *Paper*. New York, Crabtree Publishing Company, 1998.

1809. Blackhawk, Ned. *The Shoshone*. Austin, Texas, Steck-Vaughn Publishers, 2000.

1810. *Bolivia*. Danbury, Connecticut, Grolier Educational, 1999.

1811. Braman, Arlette N. *Kids Around the World Cook*. New York, John Wiley & Sons, 2000.

1812. Braman, Arlette N. *Kids Around the World Create: The Best Crafts and Activities from Many Lands*. New York, John Wiley & Sons, 1999.

1813. *Brazil*. Danbury, Connecticut, Grolier Educational, 1997.

1814. Bredeson, Carmen. *Texas*. Tarrytown, New York, Marshall Cavendish, 1997.

1815. Brill, Marlene Targ. *Illinois*. Tarrytown, New York, Marshall Cavendish, 1997.

1816. Brill, Marlene Targ. *Indiana*. Tarrytown, New York, Marshall Cavendish, 1997.

1817. Brill, Marlene Targ. *Michigan*. Tarrytown, New York, Marshall Cavendish, 1998.

1818. Broida, Marian. *Ancient Egyptians and Their Neighbors: An Activity Guide*. Chicago, Illinois, Chicago Review Press, 1999.

1819. Brownlie, Alison. *West Africa*. Austin, Texas, Steck-Vaughn Publishers, 1999.

1820. Brownrigg, Sheri. *Hearts and Crafts*. Berkely, California, Tricycle Press, 1996.

1821. Buchberg, Wendy. *Quilting Activities Across the Curriculum*. New York, Scholastic Professional Books, 1996.

1822. Butzow, Carol M. *Exploring the Environment Through Children's Literature*. Englewood, Colorado, Teacher Ideas Press, 1999.

1823. *Cambodia*. Danbury, Connecticut, Grolier Educational, 1999.

1824. Carlson, Laurie. *Colonial Kids: An Activity Guide to Life in the New World*. Chicago, Illinois, Chicago Review Press, 1997.

1825. Cotler, Amy. *The Secret Garden Cookbook*. New York, HarperCollins Publishers, 1999.

1826. Castillo, Edward D. *The Pomo*. Austin, Texas, Steck-Vaugh Publishers, 2000.

1827. Chadwick, Roxane. *Felt Board Story Times*. Fort Atkinson, Wisconsin, Alleyside Press, 1997.

1828. Chambers, Catherine. *All Saints, All Souls and Halloween*. Austin, Texas, Steck-Vaughn Publishers, 1997.

1829. Chambers, Catherine. *Carnival*. Austin, Texas, Steck-Vaughn Publishers, 1998.

1830. Chambers, Catherine. *Chinese New Year*. Austin, Texas, Steck-Vaughn Publishers, 1997.

1831. Chambers, Catherine. *Easter*. Austin, Texas, Steck-Vaughn Publishers, 1998.

1832. Chang, Perry. *Florida*. Tarrytown, New York, Marshall Cavendish, 1998.

1833. Chapman, Gillian. *The Aztecs*. Des Plaines, Illinois, Heinemann Interactive Library, 1997.

1834. Chapman, Gillian. *The Egyptians*. Des Plaines, Illinois, Heinemann Interactive Library, 1997.

1835. Chapman, Gillian. *Crafts from the Past: The Greeks*. Des Plaines, Illinois, Heinemann Interactive Library, 1998.

1836. Chicoine, Stephen. *Spain: Bridge Between Continents*. Tarrytown, New York, Marshall Cavendish, 1997.

1837. *Chile*. Danbury, Connecticut, Grolier Educational, 1999.

1838. *China*. Danbury, Connecticut, Grolier Educational, 1997.

1839. Chrisp, Peter. *Ancient Greece*. Chicago, Illinois, World Book, 1998.

1840. Chrisp, Peter. *Ancient Rome*. Chicago, Illinois, World Book, 1997.

1841. Chrisp, Peter. *The Middle Ages*. Chicago, Illinois, World Book, 1997.

1842. Chrisp, Peter. *The Roman Empire*. Chicago, Illinois, World Book, 1996.

1843. Chrisp, Peter. *Vikings*. Chicago, Illinois, World Book, 1998.

1844. *Christmas in Spain*. Chicago, Illinois, World Book, 1988.

1845. *Christmas in Switzerland*. Chicago, Illinois, World Book, 1995.

1846. Civardi, Anne. *Festival Decorations*. New York, Crabtree Publishing Co., 1998.

1847. Clark, Ann. *Hanukkah*. Austin, Texas, Steck-Vaughn Publishers, 1998.

1848. Clark, Domini. *South Africa: The Culture*. New York, Crabtree Publishers, 1999.

1849. Clark, Sara. *Benjamin Franklin*. Irving, Texas, Living History Productions, 1993.

1850. Clark, Sara. *General George Washington*. Irving, Texas, Living History Productions, 1993.

1851. Cobb, Mary. *A Sampler View of Colonial Life: With Projects Kids Can Make*. Brookfield, Connecticut, The Millbrook Press, 1999.

1852. Collins, Carolyn Strom. *My Little House Crafts Book*. New York, Harper Trophy Publishers, 1998.

1853. Cone, Molly. *The Story of Shabbat*. New York, HarperCollins Publishers, 2000.

1854. Cook, Deanna F. *Kids' Pumpkin Projects: Planting and Harvest Fun*. Charlotte, Vermont, Williamson Publishing Co., 1998.

1855. Covert, Kim. *Coast Miwok*. Mankato, Minnesota, Bridgestone Books, 1999.

1856. Covert, Kim. *Powhatan People*. Mankato, Minnesota, Bridgestone Books, 1999.

1857. Crosher, Judith. *Technology in the Time of Ancient Greece*. Austin, Texas, Steck-Vaughn Publishers, 1998.

1858. Crosher, Judith. *Technology in the Time of the Maya*. Austin, Texas, Steck-Vaughn Publishers, 1997.

1859. D'Amico, Joan. *The United States Cookbook*. New York, John Wiley & Sons, 2000.

1860. Dargie, Richard. *Castle Under Siege*. Austin, Texas, Steck-Vaughn Publishers, 1999.

1861. Dargie, Richard. *Knights and Castles*. Austin, Texas, Steck-Vaughn Publishers, 1999.

1862. Davis, Kevin. *Look What Came from Australia.* New York, Franklin Watts, 1999.

1863. Davis, Kevin. *Look What Came from Greece.* New York, Franklin Watts, 1999.

1864. Davis, Kevin. *Look What Came from the United States.* New York, Franklin Watts, 1999.

1865. Davis, Lucile. *Puerto Rico.* Danbury, Connecticut, Childrens Press, 2000.

1866. Dhilawala, Sakina. *Armenia.* Tarrytown, New York, Marshall Cavendish, 1997.

1867. DiDominicis, Lynn. *The Great Kapok Tree by Lynne Cherry.* Huntington Beach, California, Teacher Created Materials, 1997.

1868. Diehn, Gwen. *Making Books That Fly, Fold, Wrap, Hide, Pop Up, Twist and Turn.* Asheville, North Carolina, Lark Books, 1998.

1869. Dolman, Sue. *The Brambly Hedge Pattern Book.* New York, Philomel Books, 1985.

1870. Doney, Meryl. *Games.* New York, Franklin Watts, 1996.

1871. Doney, Meryl. *Jewelry.* New York, Franklin Watts, 1996.

1872. Dosier, Susan. *Civil War Cooking: The Confederacy.* Mankato, Minnesota, Blue Earth Books, 2000.

1873. Dosier, Susan. *Civil War Cooking: The Union Blue.* Mankato, Minnesota, Blue Earth Books, 2000.

1874. Dosier, Susan. *Colonial Cooking.* Mankato, Minnesota, Blue Earth Books, 2000.

1875. Drake, Jane. *The Kids' Summer Handbook.* New York, Ticknor & Fields, 1994.

1876. Dramer, Kim. *People's Republic of China.* Danbury, Connecticut, Childrens Press, 1999.

1877. Eder, Jeanne M. *Oyawin, The Makah.* Austin, Texas, Steck-Vaughn Publishers, 2000.

1878. Egger-Bovet, Howard. *U.S. Kids History Book of the American Civil War.* Boston, Massachusetts, Little Brown and Company, 1998.

1879. *Egypt.* Danbury, Connecticut, Grolier Educational, 1999.

1880. Eick, Jean. *Easter Crafts.* Elgin, Illinois, Child's World, 1999.

1881. Eick, Jean. *Halloween Crafts.* Elgin, Illinois, Child's World, 1999.

1882. Eick, Jean. *Mother's Day Crafts.* Elgin, Illinois, Child's World, 1998.

1883. Eick, Jean. *Thanksgiving Day Crafts.* Elgin, Illinois, Child's World, 1999.

1884. Eick, Jean. *Valentine's Day Crafts.* Elgin, Illinois, Child's World, 1998.

1885. Eldridge, Deborah B. *Teacher Talk: Multicultural Lesson Plans for the Elementary Classroom.* Boston, Massachusetts, Allyn and Bacon, 1997.

1886. Elish, Dan. *Vermont.* Tarrytown, New York, Marshall Cavendish, 1997.

1887. Elish, Dan. *Washington DC.* Tarrytown, New York, Marshall Cavendish, 1998.

1888. Enderlein, Cheryl L. *Christmas in Mexico.* Mankato, Minnesota, Hilltop Books, 1998.

1889. Enderlein, Cheryl L. *Christmas in the Philippines.* Mankato, Minnesota , Hilltop Books, 1998.

1890. *England.* Danbury, Connecticut, Grolier Educational, 1999.

1891. Erdosh, George. *Food and Recipes of the Civil War.* New York, Powerkids Press, 1997.

1892. Erdosh, George. *Food and Recipes of the Native Americans.* New York, Powerkids Press, 1997.

1893. Erdosh, George. *Food and Recipes of the Pilgrims.* New York, Powerkids Press, 1997.

1894. Erdosh, George. *Food and Recipes of the Revolutionary War.* New York, Powerkids Press, 1997.

1895. Erdosh, George. *Food and Recipes of the Thirteen Colonies.* New York, Powerkids Press, 1997.

1896. Erdosh, George. *Food and Recipes of the Westward Expansion.* New York, Powerkids Press, 1997.

1897. *Ethiopia.* Danbury, Connecticut, Grolier Educational, 1999.

1898. *Fall Holidays: Learning Through Literature, Grades 2-3.* Greensboro, North Carolina, The Mailbox, The Education Center, 1994.

1899. Fazio, Wende. *West Virginia.* Danbury, Connecticut, Childrens Press, 1999.

1900. Ferro, Jennifer. *Brazilian Foods and Culture.* Vero Beach, Florida, The Rourke Press, 1999.

1901. Ferro, Jennifer. *Italian Foods and Culture.* Vero Beach, Florida, The Rourke Press, 1999.

1902. Ferro, Jennifer. *Jewish Foods and Culture.* Vero Beach, Florida, The Rourke Press, 1999.

1903. Ferro, Jennifer. *Moroccan Foods and Culture.* Vero Beach, Florida, The Rourke Press, 1999.

1904. Ferro, Jennifer. *Russian Foods and Culture.* Vero Beach, Florida, The Rourke Press, 1999.

1905. Fischer, Maureen M. *Nineteenth-Century Lumber Camp Cooking*. Mankato, Minnesota, Blue Earth Books, 2001.

1906. Fisher, Aileen. *The Story of Easter*. New York, HarperCollins Publishers, 1997.

1907. Fisher, Teresa. *France*. Austin, Texas, Steck-Vaughn Publishers, 1999.

1908. Fisher, Teresa. *Japan*. Austin, Texas, Steck-Vaughn Publishers, 2000.

1909. Flack, Jerry D. *From the Land of Enchantment: Creative Teaching with Fairy Tales*. Englewood, Colorado, Teacher Ideas Press, 1997.

1910. Fleming, Maria. *Homes*. New York, Scholastic Professional Books, 1997.

1911. Forten, Charlotte. *A Free Black Girl Before the Civil War: The Diary of Charlotte Forten, 1854*. Mankato, Minnesota, Blue Earth Books, 2000.

1912. *France*. Danbury, Connecticut, Grolier Educational, 1999.

1913. Franklin, Sharon. *Mexico and Central America*. Austin, Texas, Steck-Vaughn Publishers, 1999.

1914. Franklin, Sharon. *Scandinavia*. Austin, Texas, Steck-Vaughn Publishers, 2000.

1915. Franklin, Sharon. *Southwest Pacific*. Austin, Texas, Steck-Vaughn Publishers, 1999.

1916. Fredericks, Anthony D. *More Social Studies Through Children's Literature*. Englewood, Colorado, Teacher Ideas Press, 2000.

1917. Freeburg, Kim. *Pocahontas*. Irving, Texas, Nest Entertainment, 1994.

1918. Fuhler, Carol J. *Discovering Geography of North America with Books Kids Love*. Golden, Colorado, Fulcrum Resources, 1998.

1919. Gag, Wanda. *The Girlhood Diary of Wanda Gag, 1908-1909: Portrait of a Young Artist*. Mankato, Minnesota, Blue Earth Books, 2001.

1920. Gardella, Tricia, comp. *Writers in the Kitchen*. Honesdale, Pennsylvania, Boyds Mills Press, 1998.

1921. Gascoigne, Ingrid. *Papua New Guinea*. Tarrytown, New York, Marshall Cavendish, 1998.

1922. Geeslin, Campbell. *How Nanita Learned to Make Flan*. New York, Atheneum Books for Young Readers, 1999.

1923. George, Charles. *Idaho*. Danbury, Connecticut, Childrens Press, 2000.

1924. *Germany*. Danbury, Connecticut, Grolier Educational, 1997.

1925. Gillespie, Sarah. *A Pioneer Farm Girl: The Diary of Sara Gillespie, 1877-1878*. Mankato, Minnesota, Blue Earth Books, 2000.

1926. Gillies, Judi. *The Kids Can Press Jumbo Cookbook*. Toronto, Canada, Kids Can Press, 2000.

1927. Gold, Judith. *Goldilocks and the Three Bears*. Monterey, California, Evan Moor Corporation, 1995.

1928. Gold, Judith. *Little Red Riding Hood*. Monterey, California, Evan Moor Corporation, 1995.

1929. Gold, Judith. *The Three Little Pigs*. Monterey, California, Evan Moor Corporation, 1995.

1930. Goldberg, Jake. *Hawaii*. Tarrytown, New York, Marshall Cavendish, 1998.

1931. Goodchild, Peter. *The Spark in the Stone*. Chicago, Illinois, Chicago Review Press, 1991.

1932. *Good Housekeeping Illustrated Children's Cookbook*. New York, William Morrow and Co., 1997.

1933. Goss, Gary. *Blue Moon Soup*. New York, Little, Brown and Company, 1999.

1934. Gould, Roberta. *Making Cool Crafts & Awesome Art: A Kids' Treasure Trove of Fabulous Fun*. Charlotte, Vermont, Williamson Publishing Co., 1997.

1935. Green, Jen M. *Making Mad Machines*. New York, Gloucester Press, 1992.

1936. Greenwood, Barbara. *Pioneer Thanksgiving: A Story of Harvest Celebrations in 1841*. Buffalo, New York, Kids Can Press, 1999.

1937. Griffin, Lana T. *The Navajo*. Austin, Texas, Steck-Vaughn Publishers, 2000.

1938. Griffiths, Diana. *Australia*. Milwaukee, Wisconsin, Gareth Stevens Publishing, 1999.

1939. Groner, Judith. *All About Passover*. Rockville, Maryland, KarBen Copies, 2000.

1940. Gryski, Camilla. *Let's Play: Traditional Games of Childhood*. Buffalo, New York, Kids Can Press, 1998.

1941. *Guatemala*. Danbury, Connecticut, Grolier Educational, 1999.

1942. Gunderson, Mary. *American Indian Cooking Before 1500*. Mankato, Minnesota, Blue Earth Books, 2001.

1943. Gunderson, Mary. *Cooking on the Lewis and Clark Expedition*. Mankato, Minnesota, Blue Earth Books, 2000.

1944. Gunderson, Mary. *Cowboy Cooking*. Mankato, Minnesota, Blue Earth Books, 2000.

1945. Gunderson, Mary. *Oregon Trail Cooking.* Mankato, Minnesota, Blue Earth Books, 2000.

1946. Gunderson, Mary. *Pioneer Farm Cooking.* Mankato, Minnesota, Blue Earth Books, 2000.

1947. Gunderson, Mary. *Southern Plantation Cooking.* Mankato, Minnesota, Blue Earth Books, 2000.

1948. Hamilton, Leslie. *Child's Play Around the World: 170 Crafts, Games and Projects for Two-to-Six Year-Olds.* New York, The Berkley Publishing Group, 1996.

1949. Hamilton, Leslie. *Child's Play: 200 Instant Crafts and Activities for Preschoolers.* New York, Crown Publishers, 1989.

1950. Harbison, Elizabeth M. *Loaves of Fun: A History of Bread with Activities and Recipes from Around the World.* Chicago, Illinois, Chicago Review Press, 1997.

1951. Hart, Avery. *Ancient Greece: 40 Hands-On Activities to Experience this Wonderous Age.* Charlotte, Vermont, Williamson Publishing Co., 1999.

1952. Hart, Avery. *Boredom Busters!: The Curious Kids Activity Book.* Charlotte, Vermont, Williamson Publishing Co., 1997.

1953. Hart, Avery. *Kids Garden: The Anytime, Anyplace Guide to Sowing and Growing Fun.* Charlotte, Vermont, Williamson Publishing Co., 1996.

1954. Hart, Avery. *Knights and Castles.* Charlotte, Vermont, Williamson Publishing Co., 1998.

1955. Harvey, Miles. *Look What Came from China.* Danbury, Connecticut, Franklin Watts, 1998.

1956. Harvey, Miles. *Look What Came from Egypt.* Danbury, Connecticut, Franklin Watts, 1998.

1957. Harvey, Miles. *Look What Came from France.* New York, Franklin Watts, 1999.

1958. Harvey, Miles. *Look What Came from India.* New York, Franklin Watts, 1999.

1959. Harvey, Miles. *Look What Came from Italy.* Danbury, Connecticut, Franklin Watts, 1998.

1960. Harvey, Miles. *Look What Came from Japan.* New York, Franklin Watts, 1999.

1961. Harvey, Miles. *Look What Came from Mexico.* Danbury, Connecticut, Franklin Watts, 1998.

1962. Harvey, Miles. *Look What Came from Russia.* New York, Franklin Watts, 1999.

1963. Hayden, Kate. *Plains Indians.* Chicago, Illinois, World Book, 1997.

1964. Hayes, Janelle. *One-Hour Nature Crafts.* Lincolnwood, Illinois, Publications International, 1996.

1965. Heale, Jay. *South Africa.* Milwaukee, Wisconsin, Gareth Stevens Publishing, 1998.

1966. Heale, Jay. *Tanzania.* Tarrytown, New York, Marshall Cavendish, 1998.

1967. Heath, Alan. *Common Threads: Festivals of Folklore and Literature for Schools and Libraries.* Lanham, Maryland, Scarecrow Press, 1996.

1968. Heinrichs, Ann. *California.* Danbury, Connecticut, Childrens Press, 1998.

1969. Heinrichs, Ann. *Florida.* Danbury, Connecticut, Childrens Press, 1998.

1970. Heinrichs, Ann. *Indiana.* Danbury, Connecticut, Childrens Press, 2000.

1971. Heinrichs, Ann. *Pennsylvania.* Danbury, Connecticut, Childrens Press, 2000.

1972. Herbert, Janis. *The Civil War for Kids: A History with 21 Activities.* Chicago, Illinois, Chicago Review Press, 1999.

1973. Herck, Alice. *The Enchanted Gardening Book: Ideas for Using Plants to Beautify Your World, Both Indoors and Out.* New York, Random House, 1997.

1974. Hester, Sallie. *A Covered Wagon Girl, the Diary of Sallie Hester, 1849-1850.* Mankato, Minnesota, Blue Earth Books, 2000.

1975. Hewitt, Sally. *The Aztecs.* Danbury, Connecticut, Childrens Press, 1996.

1976. Hewitt, Sally. *The Greeks.* Chicago, Illinois, Childrens Press, 1995.

1977. Hewitt, Sally. *The Plains People.* Danbury, Connecticut, Childrens Press, 1996.

1978. Hewitt, Sally. *The Romans.* Chicago, Illinois, Childrens Press, 1995.

1979. Hicks, Peter. *How Castles Were Built.* Austin, Texas, Steck-Vaughn Publishers, 1999.

1980. Hicks, Peter. *Technology in the Time of the Vikings.* Austin, Texas, Steck-Vaughn Publishers, 1997.

1981. Hintz, Martin. *Iowa.* Danbury, Connecticut, Childrens Press, 2000.

1982. Hintz, Martin. *Louisiana.* Danbury, Connecticut, Childrens Press, 1998.

1983. Hintz, Martin. *Michigan.* Danbury, Connecticut, Childrens Press, 1999.

1984. Hintz, Martin. *Minnesota.* Danbury, Connecticut, Childrens Press, 2000.

1985. Hintz, Martin. *North Carolina.* Danbury, Connecticut, Childrens Press, 1998.

1986. Hintz, Martin. *North Dakota.* Danbury, Connecticut, Childrens Press, 2000.

1987. Hirst, Mike. *India.* Austin, Texas, Steck-Vaughn Publishers, 1999.

1988. Ho, Siow Yen. *South Korea*. Milwaukee, Wisconsin, Gareth Stevens Publishing, 1998.

1989. Hoffman, Nancy. *West Virginia*. Tarrytown, New York, Marshall Cavendish, 1999.

1990. *Holidays and Celebrations, Grade 1*. Greensboro, North Carolina, The Education Center, 1997.

1991. *Holidays and Celebrations, Grade 2*. Greensboro, North Carolina, The Education Center, 1997.

1992. *Holidays and Celebrations, Grade 3*. Greensboro, North Carolina, The Education Center, 1997.

1993. *Holidays and Celebrations, Grade 4*. Greensboro, North Carolina, The Education Center, 1997.

1994. *Holidays and Celebrations, Grade 5*. Greensboro, North Carolina, The Education Center, 1997.

1995. Hollenbeck, Kathleen M. *Neighborhoods and Communities*. New York, Scholastic, 1997.

1996. Honan, Linda. *Spend the Day in Ancient Egypt: Projects and Activities that Bring the Past to Life*. New York, John Wiley & Sons, 1999.

1997. Honan, Linda. *Spend the Day in Ancient Greece: Projects and Activities that Bring the Past to Life*. New York, John Wiley & Sons, 1998.

1998. Howland, Naomi. *Latkes, Latkes, Good to Eat, A Chanukah Story*. New York, Clarion Books, 1999.

1999. Hughes, Meredith Sayles. *Cool As a Cucumber, Hot As a Pepper: Fruit Vegetables*. Minneapolis, Minnesota, Lerner Publications Co., 1999.

2000. Hughes, Meredith Sayles. *Glorious Grasses: The Grains*. Minneapolis, Minnesota, Lerner Publications Co., 1999.

2001. Hughes, Meredith Sayles. *Spill the Beans and Pass the Peanuts: Legumes*. Minneapolis, Minnesota, Lerner Publications Co., 1999.

2002. Hughes, Meredith Sayles. *Yes, We Have Bananas, Fruits from Shrubs and Vines*. Minneapolis, Minnesota, Lerner Publications Co., 2000.

2003. Ichord, Loretta Frances. *Hasty Pudding, Johnnycakes and other Good Stuff: Cooking in Colonial America*. Brookfield, Connecticut, The Millbrook Press, 1998.

2004. Illsley, Linda. *The Caribbean*. Austin, Texas, Steck-Vaughn Publishers, 1999.

2005. Illsley, Linda. *Mexico*. Austin, Texas, Steck-Vaughn Publishers, 1999.

2006. *In the Rainforest*. Monterey, California, Evan Moor Corp., 1993.

2007. *India*. Danbury, Connecticut, Grolier Educational, 1997.

2008. Ingram, W. Scott. *Oregon*. Danbury, Connecticut, Childrens Press, 2000.

2009. *Ireland*. Danbury, Connecticut, Grolier Educational, 1997.

2010. Irwin, Margaret. *My Little House Sewing Book*. New York, HarperCollins Publishers, 1997.

2011. *Israel*. Danbury, Connecticut, Grolier Educational, 1999.

2012. *Italy*. Danbury, Connecticut, Grolier Educational, 1997.

2013. Jackson, Ellen B. *The Autumn Equinox: Celebrating the Harvest*. Brookfield, Connecticut, The Millbrook Press, 2000.

2014. Jackson, Ellen. *Meeting the Millennium, Looking Back, Looking Forward: 30 Activities for the Turn of the Century*. Watertown, Massachusetts, Charlesbridge Publishing, 1999.

2015. *Jamaica*. Danbury, Connecticut, Grolier Educational, 1997.

2016. *Japan*. Danbury, Connecticut, Grolier Educational, 1997.

2017. Jermyn, Leslie. *Peru*. Milwaukee, Wisconsin, Gareth Stevens Publishing, 1998.

2018. Johnson, M. G. Ron. *Alexander Graham Bell*. Irving, Texas, Nest Entertainment, 1995.

2019. Hughes, Meredith Sayles. *Stinky and Stringy: Stem and Bulb Vegetables*. Minneapolis, Minnesota, Lerner Publications Co., 1999.

2020. Johnson, M. G. Ron. *Harriet Tubman*. Irving, Texas, Nest Entertainment, 1996.

2021. Johnson, M. G. Ron. *Helen Keller*. Irving, Texas, Nest Entertainment, 1996.

2022. Johnson, M. G. Ron. *Joan of Arc*. Irving, Texas, Nest Entertainment, 1996.

2023. Johnson, M. G. Ron. *Maccabees, The Story of Hanukkah*. Irving, Texas, Nest Entertainment, 1995.

2024. Johnson, M. G. Ron. *Marco Polo*. Irving, Texas, Nest Entertainment, 1997.

2025. Johnson, M. G. Ron. *Marie Curie*. Irving, Texas, Nest Entertainment, 1997.

2026. Johnson, M. G. Ron. *The Wright Brothers*. Irving, Texas, Nest Entertainment, 1996.

2027. Jones, Judith. *Knead It, Punch It, Bake It*. 2nd Ed. New York, Houghton Mifflin Co., 1998.

2028. *Josefina's Cookbook*. Middleton, Wisconsin, Pleasant Company Publications, 1998.

2029. *Josefina's Craft Book*. Middleton, Wisconsin, Pleasant Company Publications, 1998.

2030. Jurenka, Nancy Allen. *Cultivating a Child's Imagination Through Gardening.* Englewood, Colorado, Teacher Ideas Press, 1996.

2031. Kadodwala, Dilip. *Holi.* Austin, Texas, Steck-Vaughn Publishers, 1997.

2032. Kairi, Wambui. *Kenya.* Austin, Texas, Steck-Vaughn Publishers, 1999.

2033. Kalman, Bobbie. *Canada: The Culture.* New York, Crabtree Publishing Co., 1993.

2034. Kalman, Bobbie. *Greece: The Culture.* New York, Crabtree Publishing Co., 1999.

2035. Kalman, Bobbie. *Mexico: The Culture.* New York, Crabtree Publishing Co., 1993.

2036. Kalman, Bobbie. *Peru: The People and Culture.* New York, Crabtree Publishing Co., 1994.

2037. Kalman, Bobbie. *Vietnam: The Culture.* New York, Crabtree Publishing Co., 1996.

2038. Kavasch, E. Barrie. *The Seminoles.* Austin, Texas, Steck-Vaughn Publishers, 1999.

2039. Kent, Deborah. *Maine.* Danbury, Connecticut, Childrens Press, 1999.

2040. Kent, Deborah. *Utah.* Danbury, Connecticut, Childrens Press, 2000.

2041. Alcott, Louisa May. *The Girlhood Diary of Louisa May Alcott, 1843-1846: Writings of a Young Author.* Mankato, Minnesota, Blue Earth Books, 2001.

2042. Kerven, Rosalind. *Id-ul-Fitr.* Austin, Texas, Steck-Vaughn Publishers, 1997.

2043. King, David C. *Civil War Days: Discover the Past with Exciting Projects, Games, Activities and Recipes.* New York, John Wiley & Sons, 1999.

2044. King, David C. *Colonial Days: Discover the Past with Fun Projects, Games, Activities and Recipes.* New York, John Wiley & Sons, 1998.

2045. King, David C. *Egypt: Ancient Traditions, Modern Hopes.* Tarrytown, New York, Marshall Cavendish, 1997.

2046. King, David C. *Victorian Days: Discover the Past with Fun Projects, Games, Activities and Recipes.* New York, John Wiley & Sons, 2000.

2047. King, Penny. *Landscapes.* New York, Crabtree Publishing Co., 1996.

2048. King, Penny. *Myths and Legends.* New York, Crabtree Publishing Co., 1997.

2049. King, Penny. *Portraits.* New York, Crabtree Publishing Co., 1996.

2050. King, Penny. *Sports and Games.* New York, Crabtree Publishing Co., 1997.

2051. King, Penny. *Stories.* New York, Crabtree Publishing Co., 1996.

2052. Klein, Ted. *Rhode Island.* Tarrytown, New York, Marshall Cavendish, 1999.

2053. Kohl, Mary Ann F. *Cooking Art.* Beltsville, Maryland, Gryphon House, 1997.

2054. Kohl, Mary Ann F. *Global Art: Activities, Projects and Inventions from Around the World.* Beltsville, Maryland, Gryphon House, 1998.

2055. Kohl, Mary Ann F. *Preschool Art.* Beltsville, Maryland, Gryphon House, 1994.

2056. *Korea.* Danbury, Connecticut, Grolier Educational, 1997.

2057. Kott, Jennifer. *Nicaragua.* Tarrytown, New York, Marshall Cavendish, 1995.

2058. Kourempis-Cowling, Tania. *Cooking with Kids: Recipes for Year-Round Fun.* Torrance, California, Fearon Teacher Aids, 1999.

2059. Kourempis-Cowling, Tania. *Crafts for all Seasons: A Hands-On Celebration of Seasonal Craft Activities.* Torrance, California, Fearon Teacher Aids, 1997.

2060. Kraus, Anne Marie. *Folktale Themes and Activities for Children, Pourquois Tales, Volume 1.* Englewood, Colorado, Teacher Ideas Press, 1998.

2061. Kraus, Anne Marie. *Folktale Themes and Activities for Children, Trickster and Transformation Tales, Volume 2.* Englewood, Colorado, Teacher Ideas Press, 1999.

2062. Ladd, Edmund J. *The Zuni.* Austin, Texas, Steck-Vaughn Publishers, 2000.

2063. Lassieur, Allison. *The Inuit.* Mankato, Minnesota, Bridgestone Books, 2000.

2064. Lassieur, Allison. *The Nez Perce Tribe.* Mankato, Minnesota, Bridgestone Books, 2000.

2065. *Lebanon.* Danbury, Connecticut, Grolier Educational, 1999.

2066. LeVert, Suzanne. *Louisiana.* Tarrytown, New York, Marshall Cavendish, 1997.

2067. LeVert, Suzanne. *Massachusetts.* Tarrytown, New York, Marshall Cavendish, 2000.

2068. Levy, Patricia. *Belarus.* Tarrytown, New York, Marshall Cavendish, 1998.

2069. Levy, Patricia. *Liberia.* Tarrytown, New York, Marshall Cavendish, 1998.

2070. Lohnes, Marilyn. *Finger Folk.* Fort Atkinson, Wisconsin, Alleyside Press, 1999.

2071. Lord, Suzanne. *The Story of the Dream Catcher and Other Native American Crafts and Artwork.* New York, Scholastic, 1995.

2072. Love, Ann. *The Kids Guide to the Millennium.* Buffalo, New York, Kids Can Press, 1998.

2073. Lovejoy, Sharon. *Roots, Shoots, Buckets and Boots: Gardening Together with Children*. New York, Workman Publishing Co., 1999.

2074. Lund, Bill. *Apache Indians*. Mankato, Minnesota, Bridgestone Books, 1998.

2075. Lund, Bill. *Cherokee Indians*. Mankato, Minnesota, Bridgestone Books, 1997.

2076. Lund, Bill. *Chumash Indians*. Mankato, Minnesota, Bridgestone Books, 1998.

2077. Lund, Bill. *The Comanche Indians*. Mankato, Minnesota, Bridgestone Books, 1998.

2078. Lund, Bill. *Iroquois Indians*. Mankato, Minnesota, Bridgestone Books, 1997.

2079. Lund, Bill. *Ojibwa Indians*. Mankato, Minnesota, Bridgestone Books, 1997.

2080. Lund, Bill. *Pomo Indians*. Mankato, Minnesota, Bridgestone Books, 1997.

2081. Lund, Bill. *The Seminole Indians*. Mankato, Minnesota, Bridgestone Books, 1997.

2082. Lund, Bill. *Sioux Indians*. Mankato, Minnesota, Bridgestone Books, 1998.

2083. Lund, Bill. *Wampanoag Indians*. Mankato, Minnesota, Bridgestone Books, 1998.

2084. MacDonald, Beth. *Bible Fun for Everyone*. Canby, Oregon, Hot Off the Press, 1997.

2085. MacLeod, Elizabeth. *Bake It and Build It*. Buffalo, New York, Kids Can Press, 1998.

2086. *Mailbox Cooking with Your Kids*. Greensboro, North Carolina, The Education Center, 1997.

2087. *Mailbox Creative Crafts for Year-Round Fun, Grades K-6*. Greensboro, North Carolina, The Education Center, 1993.

2088. *Mailbox Superbook, Preschool*. Greensboro, North Carolina, The Education Center, 1998.

2089. *Mailbox Superbook, Kindergarten*. Greensboro, North Carolina, The Education Center, 1998.

2090. *Mailbox Superbook, Grade 1*. Greensboro, North Carolina, The Education Center, 1997.

2091. *Mailbox Superbook, Grade 2*. Greensboro, North Carolina, The Education Center, 1998.

2092. *Mailbox Superbook, Grade 4*. Greensboro, North Carolina, The Education Center, 1997.

2093. *Mailbox Superbook, Grade 5*. Greensboro, North Carolina, The Education Center, 1998.

2094. *Mailbox. The Best of the Mailbox Arts and Crafts, Grades K-6*. Greensboro, North Carolina, The Education Center, 1995.

2095. *Mailbox. The Best of the Mailbox, Book 2, Preschool-Kindergarten*. Greensboro, North Carolina, The Education Center, 1996.

2096. Mandell, Muriel. *Simple Experiments in Time with Everyday Materials*. New York, Sterling Publishing Co., 1997.

2097. Markham, Lois. *Colombia: The Gateway to South America*. New York, Benchmark Books, 1997.

2098. Kadodwala, Dilip. *Divali*. Austin, Texas, Steck-Vaughn Publishers, 1998.

2099. Marx, Pamela. *Travel-the-World Cookbook*. Glenview, Illinois, Good Year Books, 1996.

2100. Masters, Nancy Robinson. *Georgia*. Danbury, Connecticut, Childrens Press, 1999.

2101. McAmis, Herb. *The Cherokee*. Austin, Texas, Steck-Vaughn Publishers, 2000.

2102. McDaniel, Melissa. *South Dakota*. Tarrytown, New York, Marshall Cavendish, 1998.

2103. McKay, Patricia. *Ireland*. Milwaukee, Wisconsin, Gareth Stevens Publishing, 1998.

2104. McNair, Sylvia. *Massachusetts*. Danbury, Connecticut, Childrens Press, 1998.

2105. McNair, Sylvia. *Nebraska*. Danbury, Connecticut, Childrens Press, 1999.

2106. McNair, Sylvia. *Rhode Island*. Danbury, Connecticut, Childrens Press, 2000.

2107. Mellett, Peter. *Pyramids*. Milwaukee, Wisconsin, Gareth Stevens Publishing, 1999.

2108. Merrill, Yvonne Y. *Hands-On Asia: Art Activities for All Ages*. Salt Lake City, Utah, Kits Publishing, 1999.

2109. Merrill, Yvonne Y. *Hands-On Latin America: Art Activities for All Ages*. Salt Lake City, Utah, Kits Publishing, 1997.

2110. Merrill, Yvonne Y. *Hands-On Rocky Mountains: Art Activities About Anasazi, American Indians, Settlers, Trappers and Cowboys*. Salt Lake City, Utah, Kits Publishing, 1996.

2111. *Mexico*. Danbury, Connecticut, Grolier Educational, 1997.

2112. Miller, Marilyn. *Thanksgiving*. Austin, Texas, Steck-Vaughn Publishers, 1998.

2113. Miller, Wanda Jansen. *U.S. History Through Children's Literature: From the Colonial Period to World War II*. Englewood, Colorado, Teacher Ideas Press, 1997.

2114. Milord, Susan. *Mexico: 40 Activities to Experience Mexico, Past and Present*. Charlotte, Vermont, Williamson Publishing Co., 1998.

2115. Modesitt, Jeanne. *It's Hanukkah*. New York, Holiday House, 1999.

2116. Morgan, Nina. *Technology in the Time of the Aztecs*. Austin, Texas, Steck-Vaughn Publishers, 1998.

2117. Morrice, Polly. *Iowa*. Tarrytown, New York, Marshall Cavendish, 1998.

2118. Moscovitch, Arlene. *Egypt, The People*. New York, Crabtree Publishing Co., 2000.

2119. Needham, Bobbe. *Ecology Crafts for Kids: 50 Great Ways to Make Friends with Planet Earth*. New York, Sterling Publishing Co., 1998.

2120. NgCheong-Lum, Roseline. *Tahiti*. Tarrytown, New York, Marshall Cavendish, 1997.

2121. Nickles, Greg. *Russia, The People*. New York, Crabtree Publishing Co., 2000.

2122. *Nigeria*. Danbury, Connecticut, Grolier Educational, 1997.

2123. Owhonda, John. *Nigeria: A Nation of Many Peoples*. Parsippany, New Jersey, Dillon Press, 1998.

2124. *Pakistan*. Danbury, Connecticut, Grolier Educational, 1990.

2125. Parrella, Deborah. *Project Seasons*. Shelburne, Vermont, Shelburne Farms, 1995.

2126. Pasqua, Sandra M. *The Navajo Nation*. Mankato, Minnesota, Bridgestone Books, 2000.

2127. *Peru*. Danbury, Connecticut, Grolier Educational, 1997.

2128. Pfiffner, George. *Earth-Friendly Holidays: How to Make Fabulous Gifts and Decorations from Reusable Objects*. New York, John Wiley & Sons, 1995.

2129. Pirotta, Saviour. *Italy*. Austin, Texas, Steck-Vaughn Publishers, 1999.

2130. *Poland*. Danbury, Connecticut, Grolier Educational, 1999.

2131. *Puerto Rico*. Danbury, Connecticut, Grolier Educational, 1999.

2132. Rabe, Monica. *Sweden*. Milwaukee, Wisconsin, Gareth Stevens Publishing, 1998.

2133. Randall, Ronne. *Israel*. Austin, Texas, Steck-Vaughn Publishers, 1999.

2134. Reedy, Jerry. *Oklahoma*. Danbury, Connecticut, Childrens Press, 1998.

2135. Reid, Struan. *Castle Life*. Austin, Texas, Steck-Vaughn Publishers, 1999.

2136. Rich, Susan. *Africa: South of the Sahara*. Austin, Texas, Steck-Vaughn Publishers, 1999.

2137. Richards, Caroline. *A Nineteenth-Century Schoolgirl: The Diary of Caroline Cowles Richards, 1852-1854*. Mankato, Minnesota, Blue Earth Books, 2000.

2138. Ridgwell, Jenny. *Fruit and Vegetables*. Des Plaines, Illinois, Heinemann Library, 1998.

2139. Robinson, Dindy. *World Cultures Through Art Activities*. Englewood, Colorado, Teacher Ideas Press, 1996.

2140. Roche, Denis. *Art Around the World: Loo-Loo, Boo, and More Art You Can Do*. Boston, Massachusetts, Houghton Mifflin Co., 1998.

2141. Roeglin, Kris. *Munchies, Meals and Mayhem*. Eden Prairie, Minnesota, Wooden Spoon Publishing, 1996.

2142. Rogers, Lura. *The Dominican Republic*. Danbury, Connecticut, Childrens Press, 1999.

2143. Roop, Peter. *Let's Celebrate Halloween*. Brookfield, Connecticut, The Millbrook Press, 1997.

2144. Roop, Peter. *Let's Celebrate Thanksgiving*. Brookfield, Connecticut, The Millbrook Press, 1999.

2145. Roraff, Susan. *Chile*. Milwaukee, Wisconsin, Gareth Stevens Publishing, 1998.

2146. Ross, Kathy. *Crafts from Your Favorite Bible Stories*. Brookfield, Connecticut, The Millbrook Press, 2000.

2147. Ross, Kathy. *Crafts for Kids Who are Wild About Deserts*. Brookfield, Connecticut, The Millbrook Press, 1998.

2148. Rose, David. *Passover*. Austin, Texas, Steck-Vaughn Publishers, 1997.

2149. Ross, Kathy. *Crafts for Kids Who are Wild About Polar Life*. Brookfield, Connecticut, The Millbrook Press, 1998.

2150. Ross, Kathy. *Crafts for St. Patrick's Day*. Brookfield, Connecticut, The Millbrook Press, 1999.

2151. Ross, Kathy. *Crafts to Make in the Fall*. Brookfield, Connecticut, The Millbrook Press, 1998.

2152. Ross, Kathy. *Crafts to Make in the Spring*. Brookfield, Connecticut, The Millbrook Press, 1998.

2153. Ross, Kathy. *Crafts to Make in the Winter*. Brookfield, Connecticut, The Millbrook Press, 1999.

2154. Ross, Kathy. *The Jewish Holiday Craft Book*. Brookfield, Connecticut, The Millbrook Press, 1997.

2155. Ross, Pamela. *Chinook People*. Mankato, Minnesota, Bridgestone Books, 1999.

2156. Ross, Pamela. *Pueblo Indians*. Mankato, Minnesota, Bridgestone Books, 1999.

2157. Rupp, Rebecca. *Everything You Never Learned About Birds*. Pownal, Vermont, Storey Communications, 1995.

2158. *Russia*. Danbury, Connecticut, Grolier Educational, 1997.

2159. Rybak, Sharon. *Tomi dePaola in the Classroom*. Torrance, California, Good Apple, 1993.

2160. Sabbeth, Carol. *Crayons and Computers*. Chicago, Illinois, Chicago Review Press, 1998.

2161. Sadler, Judy Ann. *The Kids Can Press Jumbo Book of Crafts*. Toronto, Ontario, Kids Can Press, 1997.

2162. Santella, Andrew. *Illinois*. Danbury, Connecticut, Childrens Press, 1998.

2163. Sarquis, Mickey. *Science Projects for Holidays Throughout the Year*. Middletown, Ohio, Terrific Science Press, 1999.

2164. Schomp, Virginia. *New York*. Tarrytown, New York, Marshall Cavendish, 1997.

2165. Schotter, Roni. *Purim Play*. New York, Little Brown and Co., 1998.

2166. Schroeder, Lisa Golden. *California Gold Rush Cooking*. Mankato, Minnesota, Blue Earth Books, 2001.

2167. Serra. Mariana. *Brazil*. Austin, Texas, Steck-Vaughn Publishers, 2000.

2168. Sevaly, Karen. *Spring Idea Book*. Riverside, California, Teacher's Friend Publications, 1990.

2169. Sheehan, Sean. *Guatemala*. Tarrytown, New York, Marshall Cavendish, 1998.

2170. Sherrow, Victoria. *Connecticut*. Tarrytown, New York, Marshall Cavendish, 1998.

2171. Sherrow, Victoria. *Ohio*. Tarrytown, New York, Marshall Cavendish, 1999.

2172. Shui, Amy. *China*. Austin, Texas, Steck-Vaughn Publishers, 1999.

2173. Simon, Norma. *The Story of Passover*. New York, HarperCollins Publishers, 1997.

2174. Sioras, Efstathia. *Greece*. Milwaukee, Minnesota, Gareth Stevens Publishing, 1998.

2175. Skrepcinski, Denice. *Silly Celebrations: Activities for the Strangest Holidays You've Never Heard Of*. New York, Simon & Schuster, 1998.

2176. Smelt, Roselynn. *New Zealand*. Tarrytown, New York, Marshall Cavendish, 1998.

2177. Smith, Debbie. *Israel: The Culture*. New York, Crabtree Publishing Co., 1999.

2178. Smith, Thomasina. *Crafty Masks*. Milwaukee, Wisconsin, Gareth Stevens Publishing, 1999.

2179. Smith, Thomasina. *Crafty Puppets*. Milwaukee, Wisconsin, Gareth Stevens Publishing, 1999.

2180. Snedden, Robert. *Technology in the Time of Ancient Rome*. Austin, Texas, Steck-Vaughn Publishers, 1998.

2181. *Spain*. Danbury, Connecticut, Grolier Educational, 1999.

2182. Spann, Mary Beth. *Literature-Based Multicultural Activities*. New York, Scholastic Inc., 1992.

2183. *Spring Holidays: Learning Through Literature, Kindergarten-Grade 1*. Greensboro, North Carolina, The Education Center, 1997.

2184. Staino, Patricia A. *Arts and Crafts with Your Kids Ages 5-10*. Greensboro, North Carolina, The Education Center, 1997.

2185. Staino, Patricia A. *Holidays and Celebrations with Your Kids Ages 5-10*. Greensboro, North Carolina, The Education Center, 1997.

2186. Stalcup, Ann. *Ukrainian Egg Decoration: A Holiday Tradition*. New York, Rosen Publishing Group, 1999.

2187. Steele, Philip. *Clothes and Crafts in Ancient Greece*. Parsippany, New Jersey, Dillon Press, 1998.

2188. Number Not Used.

2189. Stefoff, Rebecca. *Alaska*. Tarrytown, New York, Marshall Cavendish, 1998.

2190. Stefoff, Rebecca. *Idaho*. Tarrytown, New York, Marshall Cavendish, 2000.

2191. Stefoff, Rebecca. *Oregon*. Tarrytown, New York, Marshall Cavendish, 1997.

2192. Stefoff, Rebecca. *Washington*. Tarrytown, New York, Marshall Cavendish, 1999.

2193. Stein, R. Conrad. *Kentucky*. Danbury, Connecticut, Childrens Press, 1999.

2194. Stein, R. Conrad. *Nevada*. Danbury, Connecticut, Childrens Press, 2000.

2195. Stein, R. Conrad. *New Jersey*. Danbury, Connecticut, Childrens Press, 1998.

2196. Steins, Richard. *Hungary: Crossroads of Europe*. New York, Benchmark Books, 1997.

2197. Stephens, Laurie Bonnell. *Christopher Columbus*. Irving, Texas, Nest Entertainment, 1991.

2198. Stephens, Laurie Bonnell. *William Bradford, the First Thanksgiving*. Irving, Texas, Nest Entertainment, 1992.

2199. *Stone Soup and Other Favorite High/Scope Recipes*. Ypsilanti, Michigan, High/Scope Educational Research Foundation, 1997.

2200. Stoppleman, Monica. *Fabric*. New York, Crabtree Publishing Company, 1998.

2201. Stull, Elizabeth Crosby. *Multicultural Discovery Activities for the Elementary Grades*. West Nyack, New York, The Center of Applied Research in Education, 1994.

2202. *Sweden*. Danbury, Connecticut, Grolier Educational, 1999.

2203. Tan, Chung Lee. *Finland*. Milwaukee, Wisconsin, Gareth Stevens Publishing, 1998.

2204. Terrill, Veronica. *Big Activities for Little Hands: Fall*. Torrance, California, Good Apple, 1993.

2205. Terrill, Veronica. *Big Activities for Little Hands: Spring*. Torrance, California, Good Apple, 1993.

117

2206. Terrill, Veronica. *Big Activities for Little Hands: Summer*. Torrance, California, Good Apple, 1993.

2207. Terrill, Veronica. *Big Activities for Little Hands: Winter*. Torrance, California, Good Apple, 1993.

2208. Thoennes, Kristin. *Christmas in Norway*. Mankato, Minnesota, Hilltop Books, 1999.

2209. Thoennes, Kristin. *Israel*. Mankato, Minnesota, Bridgestone Books, 1999.

2210. Thoennes, Kristin. *Thailand*. Mankato, Minnesota, Bridgestone Books, 1999.

2211. Thomas, John E. *The Ultimate Book of Kid Concoctions*. Strongsville, Ohio, Kid Concoctions Company, 1998.

2212. Thompson, Susan Conklin. *Folk Art Tells a Story*. Englewood, Colorado, Teacher Ideas Press, 1998.

2213. Thomson, Ruth. *The Inuit*. Danbury, Connecticut, Childrens Press, 1996.

2214. Thomson, Ruth. *The Rainforest Indians*. Danbury, Connecticut, Childrens Press, 1996.

2215. Thomson, Ruth. *The Vikings*. Chicago, Illinois, Childrens Press, 1995.

2216. *Tibet*. Danbury, Connecticut, Grolier Educational, 1999.

2217. Tull, Mary. *North America*. Austin, Texas, Steck-Vaughn Publishers, 2000.

2218. Tull, Mary. *Northern Asia*. Austin, Texas, Steck-Vaughn Publishers, 1999.

2219. *Turkey*. Danbury, Connecticut, Grolier Educational, 1997.

2220. *United States*. Danbury, Connecticut, Grolier Educational, 1999.

2221. Van Rynbach, Iris. *Captain Cook's Christmas Pudding*. Honesdale, Pennsylvania, Boyds Mills Press, 1997.

2222. Vezza, Diane Simone. *Passport on a Plate: A Round the World Cookbook for Children*. New York, Simon & Schuster, 1997.

2223. *Vietnam*. Danbury, Connecticut, Grolier Educational, 1997.

2224. Walters, Anna Lee. *Pawnee Nation*. Mankato, Minnesota, Bridgestone Books, 2000.

2225. Warner, Penny. *Kids Party Cookbook*. New York, Meadowbrook Press, 1996.

2226. Warren, Jean. *Holiday Patterns*. Everett, Washington, Warren Publishing House, 1991.

2227. Warren, Jean. *Nature Patterns*. Everett, Washington, Warren Publishing House, 1990.

2228. Washington, Donna L. *The Story of Kwanzaa*. New York, HarperCollins Publishers, 1996.

2229. Waters, Kate. *Mary Geddy's Day: A Colonial Girl in Williamsburg*. New York, Scholastic Press, 1999.

2230. Watson, Carol. *Christian*. Danbury, Connecticut, Childrens Press, 1997.

2231. Webber, Desiree. *Travel the Globe: Multicultural Story Times*. Englewood, Colorado, Libraries Unlimited, 1998.

2232. Weber, Judith Eichler. *Melting Pots: Family Stories and Recipes*. New York, Silver Moon Press, 1994.

2233. *Winter Holidays, Learning Through Literature, Grades 2-3*. Greensboro, North Carolina, The Education Center, 1993.

2234. Wister, Sally. *A Colonial Quaker Girl: The Diary of Sally Wister, 1777-1778*. Mankato, Minnesota, Blue Earth Books, 2000.

2235. Woelfle, Gretchen. *Wind at Work: An Activity Guide to Windmills*. Chicago, Illinois, Chicago Review Press, 1997.

2236. Zalben, Jane Breskin. *Leo and Blossom's Sukkah*. New York, Henry Holt and Company, 1990.

2237. Zeinert, Karen. *Wisconsin*. Tarrytown, New York, Marshall Cavendish, 1998.

2238. Zwierzynska-Coldicott, Aldona Maria. *Poland*. Milwaukee, Wisconsin, Gareth Stevens Publishing, 1998.

2239. Ferro, Jennifer. *Vietnamese Foods and Culture*. Vero Beach, Florida, The Rourke Press, 1999.

2240. Stalcup, Ann. *The Art of Native American Turquoise Jewelry*. New York, Rosen Publishing Group, 1999.

2241. Stalcup, Ann. *Japanese Origami: Paper Magic*. New York, Rosen Publishing Group, 1999.

2242. Stalcup, Ann. *Mayan Weaving: A Living Tradition*. New York, Power Kids Press, 1999.

2243. Stalcup, Ann. *Ndebele Beadwork: African Artistry*. New York, Power Kids Press, 1998.

2244. Kent, Deborah. *Wyoming*. Danbury, Connecticut, Childrens Press, 2000.

2245. Williams, John. *Water Projects*. Austin, Texas, Steck-Vaughn Publishers, 1998.

2246. Thoennes, Kristin. *Incas*. Mankato, Minnesota, Bridgestone Books, 1999.

2247. Thoennes, Kristin. *Italy*. Mankato, Minnesota, Bridgestone Books, 1999.

2248. Thoennes, Kristin. *Nigeria*. Mankato, Minnesota, Bridgestone Books, 1999.

2249. Thoennes, Kristin. *Peru*. Mankato, Minnesota, Bridgestone Books, 1999.

2250. Thoennes, Kristin. *Russia*. Mankato, Minnesota, Bridgestone Books, 1999.

Books Indexed by Author

The bold number indicates the book number. See "Books Indexed by Number" for a numerical list of books.

Alcott, Louisa May. *The Girlhood Diary of Louisa May Alcott, 1843-1846: Writings of a Young Author*. Mankato, Minnesota, Blue Earth Books, 2001, **2041**.

Altman, Linda Jacobs. *California*. Tarrytown, New York, Marshall Cavendish, 1997, **1781**.

Amazing Activities and Things to Do. New York, Anness Publishing Co., 2000, **1782**.

American Girls Party Book. Middleton, Wisconsin, Pleasant Company Publications, 1998, **1783**.

Anderson, Alan H. *Geology Crafts for Kids*. New York, Sterling Publishing Co., 1996, **1773**.

Angell, Carole S. *Celebrations Around the World: A Multicultural Handbook*. Golden, Colorado, Fulcrum Publishing, 1996, **1784**.

Arts and Crafts for Little Hands, Preschool-Grade 1. Greensboro, North Carolina, Education Center, 1997, **1785**.

Ayer, Eleanor H. *Colorado*. Tarrytown, New York, Marshall Cavendish, 1997, **1786**.

Baldwin, Guy. *Wyoming*. Tarrytown, New York, Marshall Cavendish, 1999, **1788**.

Balkwill, Richard. *Clothes and Crafts in Ancient Egypt*. Parsippany, New Jersey, Dillon Press, 1998, **1787**.

Barchers, Suzanne I. *Cooking up U.S. History: Recipes and Research to Share with Children*. 2nd ed. Englewood, Colorado, Teacher Ideas Press, 1999, **1789**.

Barchers, Suzanne I. *Holiday Storybook Stew—Cooking Through the Year with Books Kids Love*. Golden, Colorado, Fulcrum Publishing, 1998, **1790**.

Barkin, Carol. *The Holiday Handbook: Activities for Celebrating Every Season of the Year and More*. New York, Clarion Books, 1993, **1791**.

Barlas, Robert. *Jamaica*. Milwaukee, Wisconsin, Gareth Stevens Publishing, 1998, **1792**.

Barr, Marilynn G. *Storybook Patterns*. Palo Alto, California, Monday Morning Books, 1995, **1793**.

Barrett, Tracy. *Kentucky*. Tarrytown, New York, Marshall Cavendish, 1999, **1794**.

Barrett, Tracy. *Tennessee*. Tarrytown, New York, Marshall Cavendish, 1998, **1795**.

Barrett, Tracy. *Virginia*. Tarrytown, New York, Marshall Cavendish, 1997, **1796**.

Bass, Jules. *Cooking with Herb, the Vegetarian Dragon*. New York, Barefoot Books, 1999, **1797**.

Bassis, Volodymyr. *Ukraine*. Tarrytown, New York, Marshall Cavendish, 1997, **1752**.

Bastyra, Judy. *Parties for Kids*. New York, Kingfisher, 1998, **1798**.

Beaton, Clare. *Easter Activity Book*. Hauppauge, New York, Barron's Educational Series, 1996, **1765**.

Berg, Elizabeth. *Nigeria*. Milwaukee, Wisconsin, Gareth Stevens Publishing, 1998, **1799**.

Berry, Carrie. *A Confederate Girl: The Diary of Carrie Berry, 1864*. Mankato, Minnesota, Blue Earth Books, 2000, **1800**.

Binder, Amy. *Abraham Lincoln*. Irving, Texas, Living History Productions, 1993, **1801**.

Binder, Amy. *Florence Nightingale*. Irving, Texas, Nest Entertainment, 1993, **1802**.

Binder, Amy. *Thomas Edison and the Electric Light*. Irving, Texas, Living History Productions, 1993, **1803**.

Bircher, William. *A Civil War Drummer Boy: The Diary of William Bircher, 1861-1865*. Mankato, Minnesota, Blue Earth Books, 2000, **1804**.

Blackhawk, Ned. *The Shoshone*. Austin, Texas, Steck-Vaughn Publishers, 2000, **1809**.

Blashfield, Jean F. *Wisconsin*. Danbury, Connecticut, Childrens Press, 1998, **1805**.

Blau, Lisa. *Fall Is Fabulous*. Bellevue, Washington, One from the Heart Educational Resources, 1994, **1806**.

Bliss, Helen. *Models*. New York, Crabtree Publishing Company, 1998, **1807**.

Bliss, Helen. *Paper*. New York, Crabtree Publishing Company, 1998, **1808**.

Bolivia. Danbury, Connecticut, Grolier Educational, 1999, **1810**.

Bonvielain, Nancy. *The Navajos: People of the Southwest*. Brookfield, Connecticut, The Millbrook Press, 1995, **1774**.

Braman, Arlette N. *Kids Around the World Cook*. New York, John Wiley & Sons, 2000, **1811**.

Braman, Arlette N. *Kids Around the World Create: The Best Crafts and Activities from Many Lands*. New York, John Wiley & Sons, 1999, **1812**.

Brazil. Danbury, Connecticut, Grolier Educational, 1997, **1813**.

Bredeson, Carmen. *Texas*. Tarrytown, New York, Marshall Cavendish, 1997, **1814**.

Brill, Marlene Targ. *Illinois*. Tarrytown, New York, Marshall Cavendish, 1997, **1815**.

Brill, Marlene Targ. *Indiana*. Tarrytown, New York, Marshall Cavendish, 1997, **1816**.

Brill, Marlene Targ. *Michigan*. Tarrytown, New York, Marshall Cavendish, 1998, **1817**.

Broida, Marian. *Ancient Egyptians and Their Neighbors: An Activity Guide*. Chicago, Illinois, Chicago Review Press, 1999, **1818**.

Brown, Roslind Varghese. *Tunisia*. Tarrytown, New York, Marshall Cavendish, 1998, **1753**.

Brownlie, Alison. *West Africa*. Austin, Texas, Steck-Vaughn Publishers, 1999, **1819**.

Brownrigg, Sheri. *Hearts and Crafts*. Berkely, California, Tricycle Press, 1996, **1820**.

Buchberg, Wendy. *Quilting Activities Across the Curriculum*. New York, Scholastic Professional Books, 1996, **1821**.

Butzow, Carol M. *Exploring the Environment Through Children's Literature*. Englewood, Colorado, Teacher Ideas Press, 1999, **1822**.

Cambodia. Danbury, Connecticut, Grolier Educational, 1999, **1823**.

Carlson, Laurie. *Colonial Kids: An Activity Guide to Life in the New World*. Chicago, Illinois, Chicago Review Press, 1997, **1824**.

Carpenter, Mark L. *Brazil: An Awakening Giant*. 2nd ed. Parsippany, New Jersey, Dillon Press, 1998, **1751**.

Castillo, Edward D. *The Pomo*. Austin, Texas, Steck-Vaugh Publishers, 2000, **1826**.

Chadwick, Roxane. *Felt Board Story Times*. Fort Atkinson, Wisconsin, Alleyside Press, 1997, **1827**.

Chambers, Catherine. *All Saints, All Souls and Halloween*. Austin, Texas, Steck-Vaughn Publishers, 1997, **1828**.

Chambers, Catherine. *Carnival*. Austin, Texas, Steck-Vaughn Publishers, 1998, **1829**.

Chambers, Catherine. *Chinese New Year*. Austin, Texas, Steck-Vaughn Publishers, 1997, **1830**.

Chambers, Catherine. *Easter*. Austin, Texas, Steck-Vaughn Publishers, 1998, **1831**.

Chang, Perry. *Florida*. Tarrytown, New York, Marshall Cavendish, 1998, **1832**.

Chapman, Gillian. *The Aztecs*. Des Plaines, Illinois, Heinemann Interactive Library, 1997, **1833**.

Chapman, Gillian. *Crafts from the Past: The Greeks*. Des Plaines, Illinois, Heinemann Interactive Library, 1998, **1835**.

Chapman, Gillian. *The Egyptians*. Des Plaines, Illinois, Heinemann Interactive Library, 1997, **1834**.

Chicoine, Stephen. *Spain: Bridge Between Continents*. Tarrytown, New York, Marshall Cavendish, 1997, **1836**.

Chile. Danbury, Connecticut, Grolier Educational, 1999, **1837**.

China. Danbury, Connecticut, Grolier Educational, 1997, **1838**.

Chrisp, Peter. *Ancient Greece*. Chicago, Illinois, World Book, 1998, **1839**.

Chrisp, Peter. *Ancient Rome*. Chicago, Illinois, World Book, 1997, **1840**.

Chrisp, Peter. *The Middle Ages*. Chicago, Illinois, World Book, 1997, **1841**.

Chrisp, Peter. *The Roman Empire*. Chicago, Illinois, World Book, 1996, **1842**.

Chrisp, Peter. *Vikings*. Chicago, Illinois, World Book, 1998, **1843**.

Christmas in Spain. Chicago, Illinois, World Book, 1988, **1844**.

Christmas in Switzerland. Chicago, Illinois, World Book, 1995, **1845**.

Civardi, Anne. *Festival Decorations*. New York, Crabtree Publishing Co., 1998, **1846**.

Clark, Ann. *Hanukkah*. Austin, Texas, Steck-Vaughn Publishers, 1998, **1847**.

Clark, Domini. *South Africa: The Culture*. New York, Crabtree Publishers, 1999, **1848**.

Clark, Sara. *Benjamin Franklin*. Irving, Texas, Living History Productions, 1993, **1849**.

Clark, Sara. *General George Washington*. Irving, Texas, Living History Productions, 1993, **1850**.

Cobb, Mary. *A Sampler View of Colonial Life: With Projects Kids Can Make*. Brookfield, Connecticut, The Millbrook Press, 1999, **1851**.

Cody, Tod. *The Cowboy's Handbook: How to Become a Hero of the Wild West*. New York, Cobblehill Books, 1996, **1761**.

Collins, Carolyn Strom. *My Little House Crafts Book*. New York, Harper Trophy Publishers, 1998, **1852**.

Cone, Molly. *The Story of Shabbat*. New York, Harper-Collins Publishers, 2000, **1853**.

Cook, Deanna F. *Kids' Pumpkin Projects: Planting and Harvest Fun*. Charlotte, Vermont, Williamson Publishing Co., 1998, **1854**.

Cotler, Amy. *The Secret Garden Cookbook*. New York, HarperCollins Publishers, 1999, **1825**.

Covert, Kim. *Coast Miwok*. Mankato, Minnesota, Bridgestone Books, 1999, **1855**.

Covert, Kim. *Powhatan People*. Mankato, Minnesota, Bridgestone Books, 1999, **1856**.

Crosher, Judith. *Technology in the Time of Ancient Greece*. Austin, Texas, Steck-Vaughn Publishers, 1998, **1857**.

Crosher, Judith. *Technology in the Time of the Maya*. Austin, Texas, Steck-Vaughn Publishers, 1997, **1858**.

D'Amico, Joan. *The United States Cookbook*. New York, John Wiley & Sons, 2000, **1859**.

Dargie, Richard. *Castle Under Siege*. Austin, Texas, Steck-Vaughn Publishers, 1999, **1860**.

Dargie, Richard. *Knights and Castles*. Austin, Texas, Steck-Vaughn Publishers, 1999, **1861**.

Davis, Kevin. *Look What Came from Australia*. New York, Franklin Watts, 1999, **1862**.

Davis, Kevin. *Look What Came from Greece*. New York, Franklin Watts, 1999, **1863**.

Davis, Kevin. *Look What Came from the United States*. New York, Franklin Watts, 1999, **1864**.

Davis, Lucile. *Puerto Rico*. Danbury, Connecticut, Childrens Press, 2000, **1865**.

Dawson, Imogen. *Clothes and Crafts in Aztec Times*. Parsippany, New Jersey, Dillon Press, 1997, **1780**.

Dawson, Imogen. *Clothes and Crafts in the Middle Ages*. Parsippany, New Jersey, Dillon Press, 1998, **1740**.

Dhilawala, Sakina. *Armenia*. Tarrytown, New York, Marshall Cavendish, 1997, **1866**.

DiDominicis, Lynn. *The Great Kapok Tree by Lynne Cherry*. Huntington Beach, California, Teacher Created Materials, 1997, **1867**.

Diehn, Gwen. *Making Books That Fly, Fold, Wrap, Hide, Pop Up, Twist and Turn*. Asheville, North Carolina, Lark Books, 1998, **1868**.

Dolman, Sue. *The Brambly Hedge Pattern Book*. New York, Philomel Books, 1985, **1869**.

Doney, Meryl. *Games*. New York, Franklin Watts, 1996, **1870**.

Doney, Meryl. *Jewelry*. New York, Franklin Watts, 1996, **1871**.

Dosier, Susan. *Civil War Cooking: The Confederacy*. Mankato, Minnesota, Blue Earth Books, 2000, **1872**.

Dosier, Susan. *Civil War Cooking: The Union Blue*. Mankato, Minnesota, Blue Earth Books, 2000, **1873**.

Dosier, Susan. *Colonial Cooking*. Mankato, Minnesota, Blue Earth Books, 2000, **1874**.

Drake, Jane. *The Kids' Summer Handbook*. New York, Ticknor & Fields, 1994, **1875**.

Dramer, Kim. *People's Republic of China*. Danbury, Connecticut, Childrens Press, 1999, **1876**.

Eder, Jeanne M. *Oyawin, The Makah*. Austin, Texas, Steck-Vaughn Publishers, 2000, **1877**.

Egger-Bovet, Howard. *U.S. Kids History Book of the American Civil War*. Boston, Massachusetts, Little Brown and Company, 1998, **1878**.

Egypt. Danbury, Connecticut, Grolier Educational, 1999, **1879**.

Eick, Jean. *Easter Crafts*. Elgin, Illinois, Child's World, 1999, **1880**.

Eick, Jean. *Halloween Crafts*. Elgin, Illinois, Child's World, 1999, **1881**.

Eick, Jean. *Mother's Day Crafts*. Elgin, Illinois, Child's World, 1998, **1882**.

Eick, Jean. *Thanksgiving Day Crafts*. Elgin, Illinois, Child's World, 1999, **1883**.

Eick, Jean. *Valentine's Day Crafts*. Elgin, Illinois, Child's World, 1998, **1884**.

Eldridge, Deborah B. *Teacher Talk: Multicultural Lesson Plans for the Elementary Classroom*. Boston, Massachusetts, Allyn and Bacon, 1997, **1885**.

Elish, Dan. *Vermont*. Tarrytown, New York, Marshall Cavendish, 1997, **1886**.

Elish, Dan. *Washington DC*. Tarrytown, New York, Marshall Cavendish, 1998, **1887**.

Enderlein, Cheryl L. *Christmas in Mexico*. Mankato, Minnesota, Hilltop Books, 1998, **1888**.

Enderlein, Cheryl L. *Christmas in the Philippines*. Mankato, Minnesota , Hilltop Books, 1998, **1889**.

England. Danbury, Connecticut, Grolier Educational, 1999, **1890**.

Erdosh, George. *Food and Recipes of the Civil War*. New York, Powerkids Press, 1997, **1891**.

Erdosh, George. *Food and Recipes of the Native Americans*. New York, Powerkids Press, 1997, **1892**.

Erdosh, George. *Food and Recipes of the Pilgrims*. New York, Powerkids Press, 1997, **1893**.

Erdosh, George. *Food and Recipes of the Revolutionary War*. New York, Powerkids Press, 1997, **1894**.

Erdosh, George. *Food and Recipes of the Thirteen Colonies*. New York, Powerkids Press, 1997, **1895**.

Erdosh, George. *Food and Recipes of the Westward Expansion.* New York, Powerkids Press, 1997, **1896**.

Erlbach, Arlene. *Happy Birthday Everywhere.* Brookfield, Connecticut, The Millbrook Press, 1997, **1749**.

Ethiopia. Danbury, Connecticut, Grolier Educational, 1999, **1897**.

Fall Holidays: Learning Through Literature, Grades 2-3. Greensboro, North Carolina, The Mailbox, The Education Center, 1994, **1898**.

Fazio, Wende. *West Virginia.* Danbury, Connecticut, Childrens Press, 1999, **1899**.

Ferro, Jennifer. *Brazilian Foods and Culture.* Vero Beach, Florida, The Rourke Press, 1999, **1900**.

Ferro, Jennifer. *Italian Foods and Culture.* Vero Beach, Florida, The Rourke Press, 1999, **1901**.

Ferro, Jennifer. *Jewish Foods and Culture.* Vero Beach, Florida, The Rourke Press, 1999, **1902**.

Ferro, Jennifer. *Moroccan Foods and Culture.* Vero Beach, Florida, The Rourke Press, 1999, **1903**.

Ferro, Jennifer. *Russian Foods and Culture.* Vero Beach, Florida, The Rourke Press, 1999, **1904**.

Ferro, Jennifer. *Vietnamese Foods and Culture.* Vero Beach, Florida, The Rourke Press, 1999, **2239**.

Fischer, Maureen M. *Nineteenth-Century Lumber Camp Cooking.* Mankato, Minnesota, Blue Earth Books, 2001, **1905**.

Fisher, Aileen. *The Story of Easter.* New York, HarperCollins Publishers, 1997, **1906**.

Fisher, Teresa. *France.* Austin, Texas, Steck-Vaughn Publishers, 1999, **1907**.

Fisher, Teresa. *Japan.* Austin, Texas, Steck-Vaughn Publishers, 2000, **1908**.

Flack, Jerry D. *From the Land of Enchantment: Creative Teaching with Fairy Tales.* Englewood, Colorado, Teacher Ideas Press, 1997, **1909**.

Fleming, Maria. *Homes.* New York, Scholastic Professional Books, 1997, **1910**.

Forten, Charlotte. *A Free Black Girl Before the Civil War: The Diary of Charlotte Forten, 1854.* Mankato, Minnesota, Blue Earth Books, 2000, **1911**.

France. Danbury, Connecticut, Grolier Educational, 1999, **1912**.

Franklin, Sharon. *Mexico and Central America.* Austin, Texas, Steck-Vaughn Publishers, 1999, **1913**.

Franklin, Sharon. *Scandinavia.* Austin, Texas, Steck-Vaughn Publishers, 2000, **1914**.

Franklin, Sharon. *Southwest Pacific.* Austin, Texas, Steck-Vaughn Publishers, 1999, **1915**.

Fredericks, Anthony D. *More Social Studies Through Children's Literature.* Englewood, Colorado, Teacher Ideas Press, 2000, **1916**.

Freeburg, Kim. *Pocahontas.* Irving, Texas, Nest Entertainment, 1994, **1917**.

Fuhler, Carol J. *Discovering Geography of North America with Books Kids Love.* Golden, Colorado, Fulcrum Resources, 1998, **1918**.

Gag, Wanda. *The Girlhood Diary of Wanda Gag, 1908-1909: Portrait of a Young Artist.* Mankato, Minnesota, Blue Earth Books, 2001, **1919**.

Ganeri, Anita. *Buddhist.* Danbury, Connecticut, Childrens Press, 1997, **1772**.

Gardella, Tricia, comp. *Writers in the Kitchen.* Honesdale, Pennsylvania, Boyds Mills Press, 1998, **1920**.

Gascoigne, Ingrid. *Papua New Guinea.* Tarrytown, New York, Marshall Cavendish, 1998, **1921**.

Geeslin, Campbell. *How Nanita Learned to Make Flan.* New York, Atheneum Books for Young Readers, 1999, **1922**.

George, Charles. *Idaho.* Danbury, Connecticut, Childrens Press, 2000, **1923**.

Germany. Danbury, Connecticut, Grolier Educational, 1997, **1924**.

Gillespie, Sarah. *A Pioneer Farm Girl: The Diary of Sara Gillespie, 1877-1878.* Mankato, Minnesota, Blue Earth Books, 2000, **1925**.

Gillies, Judi. *The Kids Can Press Jumbo Cookbook.* Toronto, Canada, Kids Can Press, 2000, **1926**.

Gillis, Jennifer Storey. *Hearts and Crafts: Over 20 Projects for Fun-Loving Kids.* Pownal, Vermont, Storey Communications, 1994, **1748**.

Gold, Judith. *Goldilocks and the Three Bears.* Monterey, California, Evan Moor Corporation, 1995, **1927**.

Gold, Judith. *Little Red Riding Hood.* Monterey, California, Evan Moor Corporation, 1995, **1928**.

Gold, Judith. *The Three Little Pigs.* Monterey, California, Evan Moor Corporation, 1995, **1929**.

Goldberg, Jake. *Hawaii.* Tarrytown, New York, Marshall Cavendish, 1998, **1930**.

Good Housekeeping Illustrated Children's Cookbook. New York, William Morrow and Co., 1997, **1932**.

Goodchild, Peter. *The Spark in the Stone.* Chicago, Illinois, Chicago Review Press, 1991, **1931**.

Goss, Gary. *Blue Moon Soup*. New York, Little, Brown and Company, 1999, **1933**.

Gould, Roberta. *Making Cool Crafts & Awesome Art: A Kids' Treasure Trove of Fabulous Fun*. Charlotte, Vermont, Williamson Publishing Co., 1997, **1934**.

Green, Jen M. *Making Mad Machines*. New York, Gloucester Press, 1992, **1935**.

Greenwood, Barbara. *Pioneer Crafts*. Toronto, Ontario, Canada, Kids Can Press, 1997, **1746**.

Greenwood, Barbara. *Pioneer Thanksgiving: A Story of Harvest Celebrations in 1841*. Buffalo, New York, Kids Can Press, 1999, **1936**.

Griffin, Lana T. *The Navajo*. Austin, Texas, Steck-Vaughn Publishers, 2000, **1937**.

Griffiths, Diana. *Australia*. Milwaukee, Wisconsin, Gareth Stevens Publishing, 1999, **1938**.

Groner, Judith. *All About Passover*. Rockville, Maryland, KarBen Copies, 2000, **1939**.

Gryski, Camilla. *Let's Play: Traditional Games of Childhood*. Buffalo, New York, Kids Can Press, 1998, **1940**.

Guatemala. Danbury, Connecticut, Grolier Educational, 1999, **1941**.

Gunderson, Mary. *American Indian Cooking Before 1500*. Mankato, Minnesota, Blue Earth Books, 2001, **1942**.

Gunderson, Mary. *Cooking on the Lewis and Clark Expedition*. Mankato, Minnesota, Blue Earth Books, 2000, **1943**.

Gunderson, Mary. *Cowboy Cooking*. Mankato, Minnesota, Blue Earth Books, 2000, **1944**.

Gunderson, Mary. *Oregon Trail Cooking*. Mankato, Minnesota, Blue Earth Books, 2000, **1945**.

Gunderson, Mary. *Pioneer Farm Cooking*. Mankato, Minnesota, Blue Earth Books, 2000, **1946**.

Gunderson, Mary. *Southern Plantation Cooking*. Mankato, Minnesota, Blue Earth Books, 2000, **1947**.

Hamilton, Leslie. *Child's Play Around the World: 170 Crafts, Games and Projects for Two-to-Six Year-Olds*. New York, The Berkley Publishing Group, 1996, **1948**.

Hamilton, Leslie. *Child's Play: 200 Instant Crafts and Activities for Preschoolers*. New York, Crown Publishers, 1989, **1949**.

Harbison, Elizabeth M. *Loaves of Fun: A History of Bread with Activities and Recipes from Around the World*. Chicago, Illinois, Chicago Review Press, 1997, **1950**.

Hart, Avery. *Ancient Greece: 40 Hands-On Activities to Experience this Wonderous Age*.

Charlotte, Vermont, Williamson Publishing Co., 1999, **1951**.

Hart, Avery. *Boredom Busters!: The Curious Kids Activity Book*. Charlotte, Vermont, Williamson Publishing Co., 1997, **1952**.

Hart, Avery. *Kids Garden: The Anytime, Anyplace Guide to Sowing and Growing Fun*. Charlotte, Vermont, Williamson Publishing Co., 1996, **1953**.

Hart, Avery. *Knights and Castles*. Charlotte, Vermont, Williamson Publishing Co., 1998, **1954**.

Hart, Avery. *Pyramids!: 50 Hands-On Activities to Experience Ancient Egypt*. Charlotte, Vermont, Williamson Publishing Co., 1997, **1769**.

Harvey, Miles. *Look What Came from China*. Danbury, Connecticut, Franklin Watts, 1998, **1955**.

Harvey, Miles. *Look What Came from Egypt*. Danbury, Connecticut, Franklin Watts, 1998, **1956**.

Harvey, Miles. *Look What Came from France*. New York, Franklin Watts, 1999, **1957**.

Harvey, Miles. *Look What Came from India*. New York, Franklin Watts, 1999, **1958**.

Harvey, Miles. *Look What Came from Italy*. Danbury, Connecticut, Franklin Watts, 1998, **1959**.

Harvey, Miles. *Look What Came from Japan*. New York, Franklin Watts, 1999, **1960**.

Harvey, Miles. *Look What Came from Mexico*. Danbury, Connecticut, Franklin Watts, 1998, **1961**.

Harvey, Miles. *Look What Came from Russia*. New York, Franklin Watts, 1999, **1962**.

Hayden, Kate. *Plains Indians*. Chicago, Illinois, World Book, 1997, **1963**.

Hayes, Janelle. *One-Hour Nature Crafts*. Lincolnwood, Illinois, Publications International, 1996, **1964**.

Heale, Jay. *South Africa*. Milwaukee, Wisconsin, Gareth Stevens Publishing, 1998, **1965**.

Heale, Jay. *Tanzania*. Tarrytown, New York, Marshall Cavendish, 1998, **1966**.

Heath, Alan. *Common Threads: Festivals of Folklore and Literature for Schools and Libraries*. Lanham, Maryland, Scarecrow Press, 1996, **1967**.

Heath, Alan. *Windows on the World: Multicultural Festivals for Schools and Libraries*. Metuchen, New Jersey, The Scarecrow Press, 1995, **1771**.

Heinrichs, Ann. *California*. Danbury, Connecticut, Childrens Press, 1998, **1968**.

Heinrichs, Ann. *Florida*. Danbury, Connecticut, Childrens Press, 1998, **1969**.

Heinrichs, Ann. *Indiana*. Danbury, Connecticut, Childrens Press, 2000, **1970**.

Heinrichs, Ann. *Pennsylvania*. Danbury, Connecticut, Childrens Press, 2000, **1971**.

Herbert, Janis. *The Civil War for Kids: A History with 21 Activities*. Chicago, Illinois, Chicago Review Press, 1999, **1972**.

Herck, Alice. *The Enchanted Gardening Book: Ideas for Using Plants to Beautify Your World, Both Indoors and Out*. New York, Random House, 1997, **1973**.

Hester, Sallie. *A Covered Wagon Girl, the Diary of Sallie Hester, 1849-1850*. Mankato, Minnesota, Blue Earth Books, 2000, **1974**.

Hewitt, Sally. *The Aztecs*. Danbury, Connecticut, Childrens Press, 1996, **1975**.

Hewitt, Sally. *The Greeks*. Chicago, Illinois, Childrens Press, 1995, **1976**.

Hewitt, Sally. *The Plains People*. Danbury, Connecticut, Childrens Press, 1996, **1977**.

Hewitt, Sally. *The Romans*. Chicago, Illinois, Childrens Press, 1995, **1978**.

Hicks, Doris Lynn. *Flannelboard Classic Tales*. Chicago, Illinois, American Library Association, 1997, **1767**.

Hicks, Peter. *How Castles Were Built*. Austin, Texas, Steck-Vaughn Publishers, 1999, **1979**.

Hicks, Peter. *Technology in the Time of the Vikings*. Austin, Texas, Steck-Vaughn Publishers, 1997, **1980**.

Hintz, Martin. *Iowa*. Danbury, Connecticut, Childrens Press, 2000, **1981**.

Hintz, Martin. *Louisiana*. Danbury, Connecticut, Childrens Press, 1998, **1982**.

Hintz, Martin. *Michigan*. Danbury, Connecticut, Childrens Press, 1999, **1983**.

Hintz, Martin. *Minnesota*. Danbury, Connecticut, Childrens Press, 2000, **1984**.

Hintz, Martin. *North Carolina*. Danbury, Connecticut, Childrens Press, 1998, **1985**.

Hintz, Martin. *North Dakota*. Danbury, Connecticut, Childrens Press, 2000, **1986**.

Hirst, Mike. *India*. Austin, Texas, Steck-Vaughn Publishers, 1999, **1987**.

Ho, Siow Yen. *South Korea*. Milwaukee, Wisconsin, Gareth Stevens Publishing, 1998, **1988**.

Hoffman, Nancy. *West Virginia*. Tarrytown, New York, Marshall Cavendish, 1999, **1989**.

Holidays and Celebrations, Grade 1. Greensboro, North Carolina, The Education Center, 1997, **1990**.

Holidays and Celebrations, Grade 2. Greensboro, North Carolina, The Education Center, 1997, **1991**.

Holidays and Celebrations, Grade 3. Greensboro, North Carolina, The Education Center, 1997, **1992**.

Holidays and Celebrations, Grade 4. Greensboro, North Carolina, The Education Center, 1997, **1993**.

Holidays and Celebrations, Grade 5. Greensboro, North Carolina, The Education Center, 1997, **1994**.

Hollenbeck, Kathleen M. *Neighborhoods and Communities*. New York, Scholastic, 1997, **1995**.

Holmes, Timothy. *Zambia*. Tarrytown, New York, Marshall Cavendish, 1998, **1754**.

Honan, Linda. *Spend the Day in Ancient Egypt: Projects and Activities that Bring the Past to Life*. New York, John Wiley & Sons, 1999, **1996**.

Honan, Linda. *Spend the Day in Ancient Greece: Projects and Activities that Bring the Past to Life*. New York, John Wiley & Sons, 1998, **1997**.

Howland, Naomi. *Latkes, Latkes, Good to Eat, A Chanukah Story*. New York, Clarion Books, 1999, **1998**.

Hughes, Meredith Sayles. *Cool As a Cucumber, Hot As a Pepper: Fruit Vegetables*. Minneapolis, Minnesota, Lerner Publications Co., 1999, **1999**.

Hughes, Meredith Sayles. *Glorious Grasses: The Grains*. Minneapolis, Minnesota, Lerner Publications Co., 1999, **2000**.

Hughes, Meredith Sayles. *Spill the Beans and Pass the Peanuts: Legumes*. Minneapolis, Minnesota, Lerner Publications Co., 1999, **2001**.

Hughes, Meredith Sayles. *Stinky and Stringy: Stem and Bulb Vegetables*. Minneapolis, Minnesota, Lerner Publications Co., 1999, **2019**.

Hughes, Meredith Sayles. *Yes, We Have Bananas, Fruits from Shrubs and Vines*. Minneapolis, Minnesota, Lerner Publications Co., 2000, **2002**.

Ichord, Loretta Frances. *Hasty Pudding, Johnnycakes and other Good Stuff: Cooking in Colonial America*. Brookfield, Connecticut, The Millbrook Press, 1998, **2003**.

Illsley, Linda. *The Caribbean*. Austin, Texas, Steck-Vaughn Publishers, 1999, **2004**.

Illsley, Linda. *Mexico*. Austin, Texas, Steck-Vaughn Publishers, 1999, **2005**.

In the Rainforest. Monterey, California, Evan Moor Corp., 1993, **2006**.

India. Danbury, Connecticut, Grolier Educational, 1997, **2007**.

Ingram, W. Scott. *Oregon.* Danbury, Connecticut, Childrens Press, 2000, **2008**.

Ireland. Danbury, Connecticut, Grolier Educational, 1997, **2009**.

Irwin, Margaret. *My Little House Sewing Book.* New York, HarperCollins Publishers, 1997, **2010**.

Israel. Danbury, Connecticut, Grolier Educational, 1999, **2011**.

Italy. Danbury, Connecticut, Grolier Educational, 1997, **2012**.

Jackson, Ellen B. *The Autumn Equinox: Celebrating the Harvest.* Brookfield, Connecticut, The Millbrook Press, 2000, **2013**.

Jackson, Ellen. *Meeting the Millennium, Looking Back, Looking Forward: 30 Activities for the Turn of the Century.* Watertown, Massachusetts, Charlesbridge Publishing, 1999, **2014**.

Jamaica. Danbury, Connecticut, Grolier Educational, 1997, **2015**.

Japan. Danbury, Connecticut, Grolier Educational, 1997, **2016**.

Jermyn, Leslie. *Peru.* Milwaukee, Wisconsin, Gareth Stevens Publishing, 1998, **2017**.

Johnson, M. G. Ron. *Alexander Graham Bell.* Irving, Texas, Nest Entertainment, 1995, **2018**.

Johnson, M. G. Ron. *Harriet Tubman.* Irving, Texas, Nest Entertainment, 1996, **2020**.

Johnson, M. G. Ron. *Helen Keller.* Irving, Texas, Nest Entertainment, 1996, **2021**.

Johnson, M. G. Ron. *Joan of Arc.* Irving, Texas, Nest Entertainment, 1996, **2022**.

Johnson, M. G. Ron. *Maccabees, The Story of Hanukkah.* Irving, Texas, Nest Entertainment, 1995, **2023**.

Johnson, M. G. Ron. *Marco Polo.* Irving, Texas, Nest Entertainment, 1997, **2024**.

Johnson, M. G. Ron. *Marie Curie.* Irving, Texas, Nest Entertainment, 1997, **2025**.

Johnson, M. G. Ron. *The Wright Brothers.* Irving, Texas, Nest Entertainment, 1996, **2026**.

Jones, Judith. *Knead It, Punch It, Bake It.* 2nd Ed. New York, Houghton Mifflin Co., 1998, **2027**.

Josefina's Cookbook. Middleton, Wisconsin, Pleasant Company Publications, 1998, **2028**.

Josefina's Craft Book. Middleton, Wisconsin, Pleasant Company Publications, 1998, **2029**.

Jurenka, Nancy Allen. *Cultivating a Child's Imagination Through Gardening.* Englewood, Colorado, Teacher Ideas Press, 1996, **2030**.

Kadodwala, Dilip. *Divali.* Austin, Texas, Steck-Vaughn Publishers, 1998, **2098**.

Kadodwala, Dilip. *Holi.* Austin, Texas, Steck-Vaughn Publishers, 1997, **2031**.

Kagda, Falaq. *Algeria.* Tarrytown, New York, Marshall Cavendish, 1997, **1755**.

Kagda, Falaq. *Hong Kong.* Tarrytown, New York, Marshall Cavendish, 1998, **1756**.

Kagda, Sakina. *Lithuania.* Tarrytown, New York, Marshall Cavendish, 1997, **1757**.

Kairi, Wambui. *Kenya.* Austin, Texas, Steck-Vaughn Publishers, 1999, **2032**.

Kalman, Bobbie. *Canada: The Culture.* New York, Crabtree Publishing Co., 1993, **2033**.

Kalman, Bobbie. *Greece: The Culture.* New York, Crabtree Publishing Co., 1999, **2034**.

Kalman, Bobbie. *Mexico: The Culture.* New York, Crabtree Publishing Co., 1993, **2035**.

Kalman, Bobbie. *Peru: The People and Culture.* New York, Crabtree Publishing Co., 1994, **2036**.

Kalman, Bobbie. *Vietnam: The Culture.* New York, Crabtree Publishing Co., 1996, **2037**.

Kasbarian, Lucine. *Armenia, A Rugged Land, An Enduring People.* Parsippany, New Jersey, Dillon Press, 1998, **1758**.

Kavasch, E. Barrie. *The Seminoles.* Austin, Texas, Steck-Vaughn Publishers, 1999, **2038**.

Kent, Deborah. *Maine.* Danbury, Connecticut, Childrens Press, 1999, **2039**.

Kent, Deborah. *Utah.* Danbury, Connecticut, Childrens Press, 2000, **2040**.

Kent, Deborah. *Wyoming.* Danbury, Connecticut, Childrens Press, 2000, **2244**.

Kerven, Rosalind. *Id-ul-Fitr.* Austin, Texas, Steck-Vaughn Publishers, 1997, **2042**.

King, David C. *Civil War Days: Discover the Past with Exciting Projects, Games, Activities and Recipes.* New York, John Wiley & Sons, 1999, **2043**.

King, David C. *Colonial Days: Discover the Past with Fun Projects, Games, Activities and Recipes.* New York, John Wiley & Sons, 1998, **2044**.

King, David C. *Egypt: Ancient Traditions, Modern Hopes.* Tarrytown, New York, Marshall Cavendish, 1997, **2045**.

King, David C. *Pioneer Days: Discover the Past with Fun Projects, Games, Activities and Recipes.* New York, John Wiley & Sons, 1997, **1750**.

King, David C. *Victorian Days: Discover the Past with Fun Projects, Games, Activities and Recipes.* New York, John Wiley & Sons, 2000, **2046**.

King, Penny. *Landscapes*. New York, Crabtree Publishing Co., 1996, **2047**.

King, Penny. *Myths and Legends*. New York, Crabtree Publishing Co., 1997, **2048**.

King, Penny. *Portraits*. New York, Crabtree Publishing Co., 1996, **2049**.

King, Penny. *Sports and Games*. New York, Crabtree Publishing Co., 1997, **2050**.

King, Penny. *Stories*. New York, Crabtree Publishing Co., 1996, **2051**.

Klein, Ted. *Rhode Island*. Tarrytown, New York, Marshall Cavendish, 1999, **2052**.

Kohl, Mary Ann F. *Cooking Art*. Beltsville, Maryland, Gryphon House, 1997, **2053**.

Kohl, Mary Ann F. *Global Art: Activities, Projects and Inventions from Around the World*. Beltsville, Maryland, Gryphon House, 1998, **2054**.

Kohl, Mary Ann F. *Preschool Art*. Beltsville, Maryland, Gryphon House, 1994, **2055**.

Korea. Danbury, Connecticut, Grolier Educational, 1997, **2056**.

Kott, Jennifer. *Nicaragua*. Tarrytown, New York, Marshall Cavendish, 1995, **2057**.

Kourempis-Cowling, Tania. *Cooking with Kids: Recipes for Year-Round Fun*. Torrance, California, Fearon Teacher Aids, 1999, **2058**.

Kourempis-Cowling, Tania. *Crafts for all Seasons: A Hands-On Celebration of Seasonal Craft Activities*. Torrance, California, Fearon Teacher Aids, 1997, **2059**.

Kraus, Anne Marie. *Folktale Themes and Activities for Children, Pourquois Tales, Volume 1*. Englewood, Colorado, Teacher Ideas Press, 1998, **2060**.

Kraus, Anne Marie. *Folktale Themes and Activities for Children, Trickster and Transformation Tales, Volume 2*. Englewood, Colorado, Teacher Ideas Press, 1999, **2061**.

Ladd, Edmund J. *The Zuni*. Austin, Texas, Steck-Vaughn Publishers, 2000, **2062**.

Lassieur, Allison. *The Inuit*. Mankato, Minnesota, Bridgestone Books, 2000, **2063**.

Lassieur, Allison. *The Nez Perce Tribe*. Mankato, Minnesota, Bridgestone Books, 2000, **2064**.

Lebanon. Danbury, Connecticut, Grolier Educational, 1999, **2065**.

LeVert, Suzanne. *Louisiana*. Tarrytown, New York, Marshall Cavendish, 1997, **2066**.

LeVert, Suzanne. *Massachusetts*. Tarrytown, New York, Marshall Cavendish, 2000, **2067**.

Levy, Patricia. *Belarus*. Tarrytown, New York, Marshall Cavendish, 1998, **2068**.

Levy, Patricia. *Liberia*. Tarrytown, New York, Marshall Cavendish, 1998, **2069**.

Lohnes, Marilyn. *Finger Folk*. Fort Atkinson, Wisconsin, Alleyside Press, 1999, **2070**.

Lord, Suzanne. *The Story of the Dream Catcher and Other Native American Crafts and Artwork*. New York, Scholastic, 1995, **2071**.

Love, Ann. *The Kids Guide to the Millennium*. Buffalo, New York, Kids Can Press, 1998, **2072**.

Lovejoy, Sharon. *Roots, Shoots, Buckets and Boots: Gardening Together with Children*. New York, Workman Publishing Co., 1999, **2073**.

Lund, Bill. *Apache Indians*. Mankato, Minnesota, Bridgestone Books, 1998, **2074**.

Lund, Bill. *Cherokee Indians*. Mankato, Minnesota, Bridgestone Books, 1997, **2075**.

Lund, Bill. *Chumash Indians*. Mankato, Minnesota, Bridgestone Books, 1998, **2076**.

Lund, Bill. *The Comanche Indians*. Mankato, Minnesota, Bridgestone Books, 1998, **2077**.

Lund, Bill. *Iroquois Indians*. Mankato, Minnesota, Bridgestone Books, 1997, **2078**.

Lund, Bill. *Ojibwa Indians*. Mankato, Minnesota, Bridgestone Books, 1997, **2079**.

Lund, Bill. *Pomo Indians*. Mankato, Minnesota, Bridgestone Books, 1997, **2080**.

Lund, Bill. *The Seminole Indians*. Mankato, Minnesota, Bridgestone Books, 1997, **2081**.

Lund, Bill. *Sioux Indians*. Mankato, Minnesota, Bridgestone Books, 1998, **2082**.

Lund, Bill. *Wampanoag Indians*. Mankato, Minnesota, Bridgestone Books, 1998, **2083**.

MacDonald, Beth. *Bible Fun for Everyone*. Canby, Oregon, Hot Off the Press, 1997, **2084**.

MacLeod, Elizabeth. *Bake It and Build It*. Buffalo, New York, Kids Can Press, 1998, **2085**.

Mailbox Cooking with Your Kids. Greensboro, North Carolina, The Education Center, 1997, **2086**.

Mailbox Creative Crafts for Year-Round Fun, Grades K-6. Greensboro, North Carolina, The Education Center, 1993, **2087**.

Mailbox Superbook, Preschool. Greensboro, North Carolina, The Education Center, 1998, **2088**.

Mailbox Superbook, Kindergarten. Greensboro, North Carolina, The Education Center, 1998, **2089**.

Mailbox Superbook, Grade 1. Greensboro, North Carolina, The Education Center, 1997, **2090**.

Mailbox Superbook, Grade 2. Greensboro, North Carolina, The Education Center, 1998, **2091**.

Mailbox Superbook, Grade 4. Greensboro, North Carolina, The Education Center, 1997, **2092**.

Mailbox Superbook, Grade 5. Greensboro, North Carolina, The Education Center, 1998, **2093**.

Mailbox. The Best of the Mailbox Arts and Crafts, Grades K-6. Greensboro, North Carolina, The Education Center, 1995, **2094**.

Mailbox. The Best of the Mailbox, Book 2, Preschool-Kindergarten. Greensboro, North Carolina, The Education Center, 1996, **2095**.

Mallett, Jerry. *World Folktales: A Multicultural Approach to Whole Language*. Fort Atkinson, Wisconsin, Alleyside Press, 1994, **1768**.

Mandell, Muriel. *Simple Experiments in Time with Everyday Materials*. New York, Sterling Publishing Co., 1997, **2096**.

Markham, Lois. *Colombia: The Gateway to South America*. New York, Benchmark Books, 1997, **2097**.

Marx, Pamela. *Travel-the-World Cookbook*. Glenview, Illinois, Good Year Books, 1996, **2099**.

Masters, Nancy Robinson. *Georgia*. Danbury, Connecticut, Childrens Press, 1999, **2100**.

McAmis, Herb. *The Cherokee*. Austin, Texas, Steck-Vaughn Publishers, 2000, **2101**.

McDaniel, Melissa. *South Dakota*. Tarrytown, New York, Marshall Cavendish, 1998, **2102**.

McKay, Patricia. *Ireland*. Milwaukee, Wisconsin, Gareth Stevens Publishing, 1998, **2103**.

McNair, Sylvia. *Massachusetts*. Danbury, Connecticut, Childrens Press, 1998, **2104**.

McNair, Sylvia. *Nebraska*. Danbury, Connecticut, Childrens Press, 1999, **2105**.

McNair, Sylvia. *Rhode Island*. Danbury, Connecticut, Childrens Press, 2000, **2106**.

Mellett, Peter. *Pyramids*. Milwaukee, Wisconsin, Gareth Stevens Publishing, 1999, **2107**.

Merrill, Yvonne Y. *Hands-On Asia: Art Activities for All Ages*. Salt Lake City, Utah, Kits Publishing, 1999, **2108**.

Merrill, Yvonne Y. *Hands-On Latin America: Art Activities for All Ages*. Salt Lake City, Utah, Kits Publishing, 1997, **2109**.

Merrill, Yvonne Y. *Hands-On Rocky Mountains: Art Activities About Anasazi, American Indians, Settlers, Trappers and Cowboys*. Salt Lake City, Utah, Kits Publishing, 1996, **2110**.

Mexico. Danbury, Connecticut, Grolier Educational, 1997, **2111**.

Miller, Marilyn. *Thanksgiving*. Austin, Texas, Steck-Vaughn Publishers, 1998, **2112**.

Miller, Wanda Jansen. *U.S. History Through Children's Literature: From the Colonial Period to World War II*. Englewood, Colorado, Teacher Ideas Press, 1997, **2113**.

Milord, Susan. *Mexico: 40 Activities to Experience Mexico, Past and Present*. Charlotte, Vermont, Williamson Publishing Co., 1998, **2114**.

Modesitt, Jeanne. *It's Hanukkah*. New York, Holiday House, 1999, **2115**.

Morgan, Nina. *Technology in the Time of the Aztecs*. Austin, Texas, Steck-Vaughn Publishers, 1998, **2116**.

Morrice, Polly. *Iowa*. Tarrytown, New York, Marshall Cavendish, 1998, **2117**.

Moscovitch, Arlene. *Egypt, The People*. New York, Crabtree Publishing Co., 2000, **2118**.

Needham, Bobbe. *Ecology Crafts for Kids: 50 Great Ways to Make Friends with Planet Earth*. New York, Sterling Publishing Co., 1998, **2119**.

NgCheong-Lum, Roseline. *Tahiti*. Tarrytown, New York, Marshall Cavendish, 1997, **2120**.

Nickles, Greg. *Pirates*. New York, Crabtree Publishing Co., 1997, **1747**.

Nickles, Greg. *Russia, The People*. New York, Crabtree Publishing Co., 2000, **2121**.

Nigeria. Danbury, Connecticut, Grolier Educational, 1997, **2122**.

Owhonda, John. *Nigeria: A Nation of Many Peoples*. Parsippany, New Jersey, Dillon Press, 1998, **2123**.

Pakistan. Danbury, Connecticut, Grolier Educational, 1990, **2124**.

Parrella, Deborah. *Project Seasons*. Shelburne, Vermont, Shelburne Farms, 1995, **2125**.

Pasqua, Sandra M. *The Navajo Nation*. Mankato, Minnesota, Bridgestone Books, 2000, **2126**.

Peru. Danbury, Connecticut, Grolier Educational, 1997, **2127**.

Pfiffner, George. *Earth-Friendly Holidays: How to Make Fabulous Gifts and Decorations from Reusable Objects*. New York, John Wiley & Sons, 1995, **2128**.

Pirotta, Saviour. *Italy*. Austin, Texas, Steck-Vaughn Publishers, 1999, **2129**.

Poland. Danbury, Connecticut, Grolier Educational, 1999, **2130**.

Powell, Jillian. *Bread*. Austin, Texas, Steck-Vaughn Publishers, 1996, **1775**.

Powell, Jillian. *Eggs*. Austin, Texas, Steck-Vaughn Publishers, 1997, **1776**.

Powell, Jillian. *Fish*. Austin, Texas, Steck-Vaughn Publishers, 1997, **1777**.

Powell, Jillian. *Fruit*. Austin, Texas, Steck-Vaughn Publishers, 1997, **1741**.

Powell, Jillian. *Milk*. Austin, Texas, Steck-Vaughn Publishers, 1997, **1742**.

Powell, Jillian. *Pasta*. Austin, Texas, Steck-Vaughn Publishers, 1997, **1743**.

Powell, Jillian. *Potatoes*. Austin, Texas, Steck-Vaughn Publishers, 1997, **1779**.

Powell, Jillian. *Poultry*. Austin Texas, Steck-Vaughn Publishers, 1997, **1744**.

Powell, Jillian. *Rice*. Austin, Texas, Steck-Vaughn Publishers, 1997, **1745**.

Powell, Jillian. *Vegetables*. Austin, Texas, Steck-Vaughn Publishers, 1997, **1778**.

Puerto Rico. Danbury, Connecticut, Grolier Educational, 1999, **2131**.

Rabe, Monica. *Sweden*. Milwaukee, Wisconsin, Gareth Stevens Publishing, 1998, **2132**.

Randall, Ronne. *Israel*. Austin, Texas, Steck-Vaughn Publishers, 1999, **2133**.

Reedy, Jerry. *Oklahoma*. Danbury, Connecticut, Childrens Press, 1998, **2134**.

Reid, Struan. *Castle Life*. Austin, Texas, Steck-Vaughn Publishers, 1999, **2135**.

Rich, Susan. *Africa: South of the Sahara*. Austin, Texas, Steck-Vaughn Publishers, 1999, **2136**.

Richards, Caroline. *A Nineteenth-Century Schoolgirl: The Diary of Caroline Cowles Richards, 1852-1854*. Mankato, Minnesota, Blue Earth Books, 2000, **2137**.

Ridgwell, Jenny. *Fruit and Vegetables*. Des Plaines, Illinois, Heinemann Library, 1998, **2138**.

Robinson, Dindy. *World Cultures Through Art Activities*. Englewood, Colorado, Teacher Ideas Press, 1996, **2139**.

Roche, Denis. *Art Around the World: Loo-Loo, Boo, and More Art You Can Do*. Boston, Massachusetts, Houghton Mifflin Co., 1998, **2140**.

Roeglin, Kris. *Munchies, Meals and Mayhem*. Eden Prairie, Minnesota, Wooden Spoon Publishing, 1996, **2141**.

Rogers, Lura. *The Dominican Republic*. Danbury, Connecticut, Childrens Press, 1999, **2142**.

Roop, Peter. *Let's Celebrate Halloween*. Brookfield, Connecticut, The Millbrook Press, 1997, **2143**.

Roop, Peter. *Let's Celebrate Thanksgiving*. Brookfield, Connecticut, The Millbrook Press, 1999, **2144**.

Roraff, Susan. *Chile*. Milwaukee, Wisconsin, Gareth Stevens Publishing, 1998, **2145**.

Rose, David. *Passover*. Austin, Texas, Steck-Vaughn Publishers, 1997, **2148**.

Ross, Kathy. *Crafts for Kids Who are Wild About Deserts*. Brookfield, Connecticut, The Millbrook Press, 1998, **2147**.

Ross, Kathy. *Crafts for Kids Who are Wild About Polar Life*. Brookfield, Connecticut, The Millbrook Press, 1998, **2149**.

Ross, Kathy. *Crafts for St. Patrick's Day*. Brookfield, Connecticut, The Millbrook Press, 1999, **2150**.

Ross, Kathy. *Crafts from Your Favorite Bible Stories*. Brookfield, Connecticut, The Millbrook Press, 2000, **2146**.

Ross, Kathy. *Crafts from Your Favorite Fairy Tales*. Brookfield, Connecticut, The Millbrook Press, 1997, **1763**.

Ross, Kathy. *Crafts to Make in the Fall*. Brookfield, Connecticut, The Millbrook Press, 1998, **2151**.

Ross, Kathy. *Crafts to Make in the Spring*. Brookfield, Connecticut, The Millbrook Press, 1998, **2152**.

Ross, Kathy. *Crafts to Make in the Winter*. Brookfield, Connecticut, The Millbrook Press, 1999, **2153**.

Ross, Kathy. *The Jewish Holiday Craft Book*. Brookfield, Connecticut, The Millbrook Press, 1997, **2154**.

Ross, Pamela. *Chinook People*. Mankato, Minnesota, Bridgestone Books, 1999, **2155**.

Ross, Pamela. *Pueblo Indians*. Mankato, Minnesota, Bridgestone Books, 1999, **2156**.

Roundhill, Clare. *Animals*. New York, Crabtree Publishing Co., 1996, **1770**.

Rupp, Rebecca. *Everything You Never Learned About Birds*. Pownal, Vermont, Storey Communications, 1995, **2157**.

Russia. Danbury, Connecticut, Grolier Educational, 1997, **2158**.

Rybak, Sharon. *Tomi dePaola in the Classroom*. Torrance, California, Good Apple, 1993, **2159**.

Ryder, Willet. *Celebrating Diversity with Art: Thematic Projects for Every Month of the Year*. Glenview, Illinois, Good Year Books, 1995, **1739**.

Sabbeth, Carol. *Crayons and Computers*. Chicago, Illinois, Chicago Review Press, 1998, **2160**.

Sadler, Judy Ann. *The Kids Can Press Jumbo Book of Crafts*. Toronto, Ontario, Kids Can Press, 1997, **2161**.

Santella, Andrew. *Illinois*. Danbury, Connecticut, Childrens Press, 1998, **2162**.

Sarquis, Mickey. *Science Projects for Holidays Throughout the Year*. Middletown, Ohio, Terrific Science Press, 1999, **2163**.

Schneebeli-Morrell, Deborah. *Puppets*. Secaucus, New Jersey, Chartwell Books, 1994, **1764**.

Schomp, Virginia. *New York*. Tarrytown, New York, Marshall Cavendish, 1997, **2164**.

Schotter, Roni. *Purim Play*. New York, Little Brown and Co., 1998, **2165**.

Schroeder, Lisa Golden. *California Gold Rush Cooking*. Mankato, Minnesota, Blue Earth Books, 2001, **2166**.

Serra. Mariana. *Brazil*. Austin, Texas, Steck-Vaughn Publishers, 2000, **2167**.

Sevaly, Karen. *Spring Idea Book*. Riverside, California, Teacher's Friend Publications, 1990, **2168**.

Sheehan, Patricia. *Luxembourg*. Tarrytown, New York, Marshall Cavendish, 1997, **1759**.

Sheehan, Sean. *Guatemala*. Tarrytown, New York, Marshall Cavendish, 1998, **2169**.

Sherrow, Victoria. *Connecticut*. Tarrytown, New York, Marshall Cavendish, 1998, **2170**.

Sherrow, Victoria. *Ohio*. Tarrytown, New York, Marshall Cavendish, 1999, **2171**.

Shui, Amy. *China*. Austin, Texas, Steck-Vaughn Publishers, 1999, **2172**.

Simon, Norma. *The Story of Passover*. New York, HarperCollins Publishers, 1997, **2173**.

Sioras, Efstathia. *Greece*. Milwaukee, Minnesota, Gareth Stevens Publishing, 1998, **2174**.

Skrepcinski, Denice. *Silly Celebrations: Activities for the Strangest Holidays You've Never Heard Of*. New York, Simon & Schuster, 1998, **2175**.

Smelt, Roselynn. *New Zealand*. Tarrytown, New York, Marshall Cavendish, 1998, **2176**.

Smith, Debbie. *Israel: The Culture*. New York, Crabtree Publishing Co., 1999, **2177**.

Smith, Thomasina. *Crafty Masks*. Milwaukee, Wisconsin, Gareth Stevens Publishing, 1999, **2178**.

Smith, Thomasina. *Crafty Puppets*. Milwaukee, Wisconsin, Gareth Stevens Publishing, 1999, **2179**.

Snedden, Robert. *Technology in the Time of Ancient Rome*. Austin, Texas, Steck-Vaughn Publishers, 1998, **2180**.

Spain. Danbury, Connecticut, Grolier Educational, 1999, **2181**.

Spann, Mary Beth. *Literature-Based Multicultural Activities*. New York, Scholastic Inc., 1992, **2182**.

Spilling, Michael. *Georgia*. Tarrytown, New York, Marshall Cavendish, 1998, **1760**.

Spring Holidays: Learning Through Literature, Kindergarten-Grade 1. Greensboro, North Carolina, The Education Center, 1997, **2183**.

Staino, Patricia A. *Arts and Crafts with Your Kids Ages 5-10*. Greensboro, North Carolina, The Education Center, 1997, **2184**.

Staino, Patricia A. *Holidays and Celebrations with Your Kids Ages 5-10*. Greensboro, North Carolina, The Education Center, 1997, **2185**.

Stalcup, Ann. *The Art of Native American Turquoise Jewelry*. New York, Rosen Publishing Group, 1999, **2240**.

Stalcup, Ann. *Japanese Origami: Paper Magic*. New York, Rosen Publishing Group, 1999, **2241**.

Stalcup, Ann. *Mayan Weaving: A Living Tradition*. New York, Power Kids Press, 1999, **2242**.

Stalcup, Ann. *Ndebele Beadwork: African Artistry*. New York, Power Kids Press, 1998, **2243**.

Stalcup, Ann. *Ukrainian Egg Decoration: A Holiday Tradition*. New York, Rosen Publishing Group, 1999, **2186**.

Steele, Philip. *Clothes and Crafts in Ancient Greece*. Parsippany, New Jersey, Dillon Press, 1998, **2187**.

Steele, Philip. *Clothes and Crafts in Roman Times*. Parsippany, New Jersey, Dillon Press, 1997, **1737**.

Steele, Philip. *Clothes and Crafts in Victorian Times*. Parsippany, New Jersey, Dillon Press, 1998, **1738**.

Steele, Philip. *The World of Festivals*. Chicago, Illinois, Rand McNally, 1996, **1766**.

Stefoff, Rebecca. *Alaska*. Tarrytown, New York, Marshall Cavendish, 1998, **2189**.

Stefoff, Rebecca. *Idaho*. Tarrytown, New York, Marshall Cavendish, 2000, **2190**.

Stefoff, Rebecca. *Oregon*. Tarrytown, New York, Marshall Cavendish, 1997, **2191**.

Stefoff, Rebecca. *Washington*. Tarrytown, New York, Marshall Cavendish, 1999, **2192**.

Stein, R. Conrad. *Kentucky*. Danbury, Connecticut, Childrens Press, 1999, **2193**.

Stein, R. Conrad. *Nevada*. Danbury, Connecticut, Childrens Press, 2000, **2194**.

Stein, R. Conrad. *New Jersey*. Danbury, Connecticut, Childrens Press, 1998, **2195**.

Steins, Richard. *Hungary: Crossroads of Europe*. New York, Benchmark Books, 1997, **2196**.

Stephens, Laurie Bonnell. *Christopher Columbus*. Irving, Texas, Nest Entertainment, 1991, **2197**.

Stephens, Laurie Bonnell. *William Bradford, the First Thanksgiving*. Irving, Texas, Nest Entertainment, 1992, **2198**.

Stone Soup and Other Favorite High/Scope Recipes. Ypsilanti, Michigan, High/Scope Educational Research Foundation, 1997, **2199**.

Stoppleman, Monica. *Fabric*. New York, Crabtree Publishing Company, 1998, **2200**.

Stull, Elizabeth Crosby. *Multicultural Discovery Activities for the Elementary Grades*. West Nyack, New York, The Center of Applied Research in Education, 1994, **2201**.

Sweden. Danbury, Connecticut, Grolier Educational, 1999, **2202**.

Tan, Chung Lee. *Finland*. Milwaukee, Wisconsin, Gareth Stevens Publishing, 1998, **2203**.

Temko, Florence. *Traditional Crafts from Native North America*. Minneapolis, Minnesota, Lerner Publications Company, 1997, **1762**.

Terrill, Veronica. *Big Activities for Little Hands: Fall*. Torrance, California, Good Apple, 1993, **2204**.

Terrill, Veronica. *Big Activities for Little Hands: Spring*. Torrance, California, Good Apple, 1993, **2205**.

Terrill, Veronica. *Big Activities for Little Hands: Summer*. Torrance, California, Good Apple, 1993, **2206**.

Terrill, Veronica. *Big Activities for Little Hands: Winter*. Torrance, California, Good Apple, 1993, **2207**.

Thoennes, Kristin. *Christmas in Norway*. Mankato, Minnesota, Hilltop Books, 1999, **2208**.

Thoennes, Kristin. *Incas*. Mankato, Minnesota, Bridgestone Books, 1999, **2246**.

Thoennes, Kristin. *Israel*. Mankato, Minnesota, Bridgestone Books, 1999, **2209**.

Thoennes, Kristin. *Italy*. Mankato, Minnesota, Bridgestone Books, 1999, **2247**.

Thoennes, Kristin. *Nigeria*. Mankato, Minnesota, Bridgestone Books, 1999, **2248**.

Thoennes, Kristin. *Peru*. Mankato, Minnesota, Bridgestone Books, 1999, **2249**.

Thoennes, Kristin. *Russia*. Mankato, Minnesota, Bridgestone Books, 1999, **2250**.

Thoennes, Kristin. *Thailand*. Mankato, Minnesota, Bridgestone Books, 1999, **2210**.

Thomas, John E. *The Ultimate Book of Kid Concoctions*. Strongsville, Ohio, Kid Concoctions Company, 1998, **2211**.

Thompson, Susan Conklin. *Folk Art Tells a Story*. Englewood, Colorado, Teacher Ideas Press, 1998, **2212**.

Thomson, Ruth. *The Inuit*. Danbury, Connecticut, Childrens Press, 1996, **2213**.

Thomson, Ruth. *The Rainforest Indians*. Danbury, Connecticut, Childrens Press, 1996, **2214**.

Thomson, Ruth. *The Vikings*. Chicago, Illinois, Childrens Press, 1995, **2215**.

Tibet. Danbury, Connecticut, Grolier Educational, 1999, **2216**.

Tull, Mary. *North America*. Austin, Texas, Steck-Vaughn Publishers, 2000, **2217**.

Tull, Mary. *Northern Asia*. Austin, Texas, Steck-Vaughn Publishers, 1999, **2218**.

Turkey. Danbury, Connecticut, Grolier Educational, 1997, **2219**.

United States. Danbury, Connecticut, Grolier Educational, 1999, **2220**.

Van Rynbach, Iris. *Captain Cook's Christmas Pudding*. Honesdale, Pennsylvania, Boyds Mills Press, 1997, **2221**.

Vezza, Diane Simone. *Passport on a Plate: A Round the World Cookbook for Children*. New York, Simon & Schuster, 1997, **2222**.

Vietnam. Danbury, Connecticut, Grolier Educational, 1997, **2223**.

Walters, Anna Lee. *Pawnee Nation*. Mankato, Minnesota, Bridgestone Books, 2000, **2224**.

Warner, Penny. *Kids Party Cookbook*. New York, Meadowbrook Press, 1996, **2225**.

Warren, Jean. *Holiday Patterns*. Everett, Washington, Warren Publishing House, 1991, **2226**.

Warren, Jean. *Nature Patterns*. Everett, Washington, Warren Publishing House, 1990, **2227**.

Washington, Donna L. *The Story of Kwanzaa*. New York, HarperCollins Publishers, 1996, **2228**.

Waters, Kate. *Mary Geddy's Day: A Colonial Girl in Williamsburg*. New York, Scholastic Press, 1999, **2229**.

Watson, Carol. *Christian*. Danbury, Connecticut, Childrens Press, 1997, **2230**.

Webber, Desiree. *Travel the Globe: Multicultural Story Times*. Englewood, Colorado, Libraries Unlimited, 1998, **2231**.

Weber, Judith Eichler. *Melting Pots: Family Stories and Recipes*. New York, Silver Moon Press, 1994, **2232**.

Williams, John. *Water Projects*. Austin, Texas, Steck-Vaughn Publishers, 1998, **2245**.

Winter Holidays, Learning Through Literature, Grades 2-3. Greensboro, North Carolina, The Education Center, 1993, **2233**.

Wister, Sally. *A Colonial Quaker Girl: The Diary of Sally Wister, 1777-1778*. Mankato, Minnesota, Blue Earth Books, 2000, **2234**.

Woelfle, Gretchen. *Wind at Work: An Activity Guide to Windmills*. Chicago, Illinois, Chicago Review Press, 1997, **2235**.

Zalben, Jane Breskin. *Leo and Blossom's Sukkah*. New York, Henry Holt and Company, 1990, **2236**.

Zeinert, Karen. *Wisconsin*. Tarrytown, New York, Marshall Cavendish, 1998, **2237**.

Zwierzynska-Coldicott, Aldona Maria. *Poland*. Milwaukee, Wisconsin, Gareth Stevens Publishing, 1998, **2238**.